"...a devastating indictment."*

"The only political playwright in the Western World who forces that world to listen to horror, Peter Weiss stuns with his newest play, THE INVESTIGATION....Weiss is a mild, gentle, relaxed man. He likes the simple things. But when Weiss writes, he changes. Then he is total theatre; he is brilliant; he is so terrifying that everyone hears."

—*Vogue Magazine*

"In THE INVESTIGATION, Peter Weiss has written a play as horrifying yet fascinating as his previous MARAT/SADE....Weiss re-creates the horrors of the camps with the strength of first-person observation. Perhaps because the words are truths, the speeches are narrative, the play can be read with the feeling that one is seeing it. THE INVESTIGATION is an important and dramatic documentation of our times."

—*Publishers' Weekly*

"An experience not to be missed. I recommend it strongly in the conviction that the most enriching adjustment to this world lies in knowing the worst as well as the best about it."

—Tom Prideaux, *Life Magazine*

"In good measure, libraries exist so that such a book as THE INVESTIGATION may be part of our experience, to make these unspeakable acts spoken, respoken, and never allowed to happen again."

—*Library Journal*

* *The Jewish Digest*

THE INVESTIGATION
was originally pub

Also by Peter Weiss

The Persecution and Assassination of Jean-Paul
Marat as Performed by the Inmates of the Asylum
of Charenton under the Direction of the Marquis
de Sade

Published by Pocket Books

THE INVESTIGATION

A Play by

PETER WEISS

English Version by
Jon Swan and Ulu Grosbard

PUBLISHED BY POCKET BOOKS NEW YORK

THE INVESTIGATION

Atheneum edition published October, 1966

A Pocket Book edition
1st printing .... December, 1967

All inquiries concerning the rights for professional or amateur stock production should be directed to Joan Daves, 145 East 49th Street, New York, N.Y. 10017

CHARACTERS

JUDGE
PROSECUTING ATTORNEY
COUNSEL FOR THE DEFENSE
1ST WITNESS
2ND WITNESS
3RD WITNESS
4TH WITNESS
5TH WITNESS
6TH WITNESS
7TH WITNESS
8TH WITNESS
9TH WITNESS
ACCUSED #1   ADJUTANT MULKA
ACCUSED #2   BOGER
ACCUSED #3   DR CAPESIUS
ACCUSED #4   DR FRANK
ACCUSED #5   DR SCHATZ
ACCUSED #6   DR LUCAS
ACCUSED #7   KADUK
ACCUSED #8   HOFMANN
ACCUSED #9   MEDICAL ORDERLY KLEHR
ACCUSED #10 SCHERPE
ACCUSED #11 HANTL
ACCUSED #12 S.S. CORPORAL STARK
ACCUSED #13 BARETZKI
ACCUSED #14 SCHLAGE
ACCUSED #15 BISCHOF
ACCUSED #16 BROAD
ACCUSED #17 BREITWIESER
ACCUSED #18 BEDNAREK

NOTE

In the presentation of this play, no attempt should be made to reconstruct the courtroom before which the proceedings of the camp trial took place. Any such reconstruction would, in the opinion of the author, be as impossible as trying to present the camp itself on the stage.

Hundreds of witnesses appeared before the court. The confrontations of witnesses and the accused, as well as the addresses to the court by the prosecution and the replies by the counsel for the defense, were overcharged with emotion.

Only a condensation of the evidence can remain on the stage.

This condensation should contain nothing but facts. Personal experience and confrontations must be steeped in anonymity. Inasmuch as the witnesses in the play lose their names, they become mere speaking tubes. The nine witnesses sum up what hundreds expressed.

The variety of experiences can, at most, be indicated by a change of voice or bearing.

Witnesses 1 and 2 are witnesses who worked with the camp administration.

Witnesses 4 and 5 are female, the rest male witnesses from the ranks of the surviving prisoners.

Each of the 18 accused, on the other hand, represents a single and distinct figure. They bear names taken from the record of the actual trial. The fact that they bear their own names is significant, since they also did so during the time of the events under consideration, while the prisoners had lost their names.

Yet the bearers of these names should not be accused once again in this drama.

To the author, they have lent their names which, within the drama, exist as symbols of a system that implicated in its guilt many others who never appeared in court.

THE INVESTIGATION

THE SONG OF THE PLATFORM

I

JUDGE:
   The witness
   was stationmaster of the railroad station
   where the trains arrived
   How far was the station from the camp
1ST WITNESS:
   A mile and a quarter from the old army camp
   About three miles from the main camp
JUDGE:
   Did your work take you into the camp
1ST WITNESS:
   No
   I only had to make sure
   that the tracks in use were in good condition
   and that the trains arrived and departed
   according to schedule
JUDGE:
   Were you in charge of
   setting up the train schedules
1ST WITNESS:
   No
   I only had to take care of technical measures
   related to scheduling the shuttle traffic
   between the station and the camp
JUDGE:
   The record contains scheduling orders
   bearing your signature

1ST WITNESS:

It's possible that in the absence
of the officer in charge
I occasionally had to sign one

JUDGE:

Were you aware
of the purpose of the transport

1ST WITNESS:

I wasn't informed on that matter

JUDGE:

You knew
that the trains were loaded with people

1ST WITNESS:

All we were told
was that it had to do
with relocation transports
carried out under government orders

JUDGE:

Didn't it seem strange to you
that the trains returning
from the camp were always empty

1ST WITNESS:

The people forwarded
had been relocated there

PROSECUTING ATTORNEY:

At present
you hold a high executive position
in the management
of the government railways
Therefore we may assume
that you are acquainted with the equipment
and loading capacity of trains
How were the trains
that arrived in your station
equipped and loaded

2

1ST WITNESS:
>   The trains in question were freight trains
>   According to the bills of lading
>   some 60 persons were forwarded in each car

PROSECUTING ATTORNEY:
>   Were the cars freight cars
>   or were they cattle cars

1ST WITNESS:
>   Some of the cars were the kind
>   used to ship cattle

PROSECUTING ATTORNEY:
>   Were there any sanitary installations
>   in the cars

1ST WITNESS:
>   I don't know

PROSECUTING ATTORNEY:
>   How often did these trains arrive

1ST WITNESS:
>   I couldn't say

PROSECUTING ATTORNEY:
>   Did they arrive frequently

1ST WITNESS:
>   Yes
>   Sure
>   It was a very busy terminal

PROSECUTING ATTORNEY:
>   Didn't it strike you
>   that the trains
>   came from almost every country in Europe

1ST WITNESS:
>   We had so much to do
>   There wasn't any time to worry about
>   things like that

PROSECUTING ATTORNEY:
>   Did you ever wonder about

what was going to happen
to the people in those trains

1ST WITNESS:

We heard they were being shipped in
for supplementary labor

PROSECUTING ATTORNEY:

But there weren't only people fit for work
but whole families
with old people and children

1ST WITNESS:

I didn't have time
to check the contents of the trains

PROSECUTING ATTORNEY:

Where did you live

1ST WITNESS:

In the town

PROSECUTING ATTORNEY:

Who else lived there

1ST WITNESS:

The town had been cleared
of its original population
Camp officials lived there
and personnel from surrounding industries

PROSECUTING ATTORNEY:

What kind of industries were those

1ST WITNESS:

They were branch plants
of I-G Farben
Krupp and Siemens

PROSECUTING ATTORNEY:

Did you see the prisoners
who had to work there

1ST WITNESS:

I saw them
when they marched to work and back

PROSECUTING ATTORNEY:
    What condition were they in
1ST WITNESS:
    They marched in step and they sang
PROSECUTING ATTORNEY:
    You didn't hear anything
    about conditions in the camp
1ST WITNESS:
    There were so many insane rumors going
        around
    you never knew what to think
PROSECUTING ATTORNEY:
    You heard nothing
    about the annihilation of people there
1ST WITNESS:
    How could anybody believe a thing like that
JUDGE:
    The witness was responsible
    for the delivery of the freight
2ND WITNESS:
    All I had to do was
    turn the trains over to the shunting crew
JUDGE:
    What were their duties
2ND WITNESS:
    They hitched the switch engine onto the trains
    and took them on into the camp
JUDGE:
    How many people would you estimate
    were there in each car
2ND WITNESS:
    I can't provide you with any information
    on that matter
    We were strictly forbidden
    to examine the trains

JUDGE:
> Who prevented you

2ND WITNESS:
> The guards

JUDGE:
> Were there bills of lading
> for all the transports

2ND WITNESS:
> In most cases there were
> no bills attached
> There was only the number
> chalked up on the freight car

JUDGE:
> What were the numbers

2ND WITNESS:
> 60 or 80 head
> It varied

JUDGE:
> When did the trains arrive

2ND WITNESS:
> Mainly at night

PROSECUTING ATTORNEY:
> What impression did you get
> of the freight

2ND WITNESS:
> I don't understand the question

PROSECUTING ATTORNEY:
> As superintendent
> of the government railroads
> you are undoubtedly familiar
> with travel conditions
> Didn't you get some idea of conditions
> by looking in through air vents
> or by hearing sounds coming from the cars

2ND WITNESS:
> Once I saw a woman

6

holding a small child up to the air vent
and calling out
over and over
for some water
I got a pitcher of water
I started to lift it up to her
when one of the guards came over
and said
if I didn't leave at once
I would be shot

JUDGE:

How many trains would you estimate
arrived in the station daily

2ND WITNESS:

On the average a train a day
When the pressure was on
two or three

JUDGE:

How long were the trains

2ND WITNESS:

They had up to 60 cars

JUDGE:

Were you ever
in the camp

2ND WITNESS:

I went in with the switch engine once
because there was something
to clear up in the bill of lading
Just back of the entrance gate I got off
and went into the camp office
I almost didn't get out of there either
because I didn't have my pass with me

JUDGE:

Did you see anything of the camp

2ND WITNESS:

    Nothing

    I was just glad to get out of there

JUDGE:

    Did you see the chimneys

    at the end of the platform

    or the smoke and glare

2ND WITNESS:

    Yes

    I saw smoke

JUDGE:

    And what did you think

2ND WITNESS:

    I thought

    those must be the bakeries

    I had heard

    they baked bread in there day and night

    After all it was a big camp

THE SONG OF THE PLATFORM

II

3RD WITNESS:
    We traveled five days
    On the second day
    our provisions were used up
    There were 89 of us in the freight car
    Our suitcases and bundles besides
    We relieved ourselves
    in the straw
    Many were sick
    and eight were dead
    At the stations along the way
    we could look out through the air vents
    and see the women personnel
    handing food and coffee up to the guards
    Our children had stopped crying
    when on the last night we were switched
    off the main track onto a siding
    We passed through a flat region
    lit up by searchlights
    Then we came up along a very long
    building like a shed
    There was a tower
    and under it an archway
    The locomotive whistled
    before we went in under the arch
    The train stopped
    The freight-car doors were pulled open
    Prisoners in striped uniforms appeared

and yelled in at us
Out
Move
Fast
Fast
It was four feet down to the ground
The ground was broken rock
The old people and the sick fell
onto the sharp stones
The dead and the luggage
were thrown out of the cars
Then we heard
Leave everything where it is
Women and children there
Men on the other side
I lost sight of my family
All around
people were shouting for
their families their relatives
They were being beaten with clubs
Dogs were barking
Searchlights and machine guns were trained
at us from the observation towers
At the end of the platform was the sky
glowing red
The air was full of smoke
The smoke had a sweet singed smell
From then on
this smoke was always there
4TH WITNESS:
I could still hear my husband
calling me
We were lined up
and were not permitted to change places
We were a group
of 100 women and children

We stood five in a row
Then we had to walk past some officers
One of them held his hand at chest level
and pointed his finger
left then right
The children and old women
went to the left
I went to the right
The left group had to cross the tracks
to get over to a road
I saw my mother for just a second
She was in the group with the children
That made me feel a bit easier
and I thought
we'll manage to get together again
A woman next to me said
They're going to a rehabilitation camp
She pointed to the trucks
parked on the road
and a Red Cross car
We could see
them being loaded into a truck
and we were glad they could ride again
The rest of us had to go
down the muddy road on foot

5TH WITNESS:

I held my sister-in-law's child
by the hand
My sister-in-law
was holding her smallest child
in her own arms
Then one of the prisoners came up to me
and asked if the child was mine
when I said it wasn't
he said I should give it to its mother

I did and I thought
perhaps mothers got special consideration
They all went off to the left
I went to the right
The officer who divided us
was very friendly
I asked him
where the others were going
and he said
They're just going to shower now
You'll see them again in an hour

JUDGE:

Does the witness
know who this officer was

5TH WITNESS:

I found out later
that his name was Dr Capesius

JUDGE:

Can the witness tell us
which of the accused is Dr Capesius

5TH WITNESS:

When I look at their faces
I find it hard to tell
whether I recognize them or not
But that man there
looks familiar to me

JUDGE:

What is his name

5TH WITNESS:

Dr Capesius

ACCUSED #3:

The witness must have confused me
with someone else
I never took part in the selections
on the platform

6TH WITNESS:

    I had known Dr Capesius from my hometown
    I was a doctor
    and before the war
    he used to call on me frequently
    as a representative of the Bayer concern
    On the platform I greeted him and asked
    what was going to happen to us
    He said
    Everything's going to be fine here
    I told him
    my wife was not well
    Then she should stand over there
    he said
    She will receive medical attention there
    He pointed to the group
    of old people and children
    I told my wife
    You go over there and get in line
    She went over with her niece
    and a couple of other relatives
    to where the sick stood
    They were all taken away in trucks

JUDGE:

    There is no doubt in your mind
    that that man was Dr Capesius

6TH WITNESS:

    No
    I spoke with him
    At the time it was a great pleasure for me
    to see him again

JUDGE:

    Accused Capesius
    do you know this witness

ACCUSED #3:

    No

13

JUDGE:

Were you present on the platform
for the arrival of transports

ACCUSED #3:

I was only there
to receive the medical supplies
from the prisoners' luggage
I had to store these supplies
in the dispensary

JUDGE:

Whom else among the accused
did you see on the platform

6TH WITNESS:

Him
I remember his name
His name is Hofmann

JUDGE:

Accused Hofmann
what were your duties on the platform

ACCUSED #8:

I was there to keep peace and order

JUDGE:

How did you do that

ACCUSED #8:

The people were lined up
Then the doctors decided
who was fit for work
and who wasn't
Sometimes there were more
and sometimes less
The percentage was decided beforehand
It was determined by the need
for manpower at the time

JUDGE:

What happened to those
who were not used for work

ACCUSED #8:

They were gassed

JUDGE:

What percent of the people
was fit for work

ACCUSED #8:

On the average
one third of a transport
When the camp was overloaded
transports went straight through
without being opened

JUDGE:

Did you yourself
carry out any selections

ACCUSED #8:

All I can say
is that sometimes
when they begged me to
I pushed some of the unfit
over to the fit group

JUDGE:

Were you allowed to do that

ACCUSED #8:

No
It was against regulations
but we closed our eyes to it

JUDGE:

Were special rations issued
for men assigned to platform duty

ACCUSED #8:

Yes
We got bread
a portion of sausage
and a half pint of brandy

JUDGE:

    In the performance of your duties
    did you ever need to resort to force

ACCUSED #8:

    There was always a lot of confusion
    and naturally sometimes
    somebody had to be straightened out
    or slapped
    I only did my duty
    Whatever I'm assigned to do
    I do my duty

JUDGE:

    How did you get this assignment

ACCUSED #8:

    By accident
    It was like this
    My brother had an extra uniform
    I could use
    So it didn't cost me anything
    Then there were business reasons
    My father had a restaurant
    that a lot of party members used to come to
    When I was sent off
    I had no idea
    where I would end up
    When I got to the camp I asked
    Am I really in the right place
    They told me
    You're in the right place here all right

PROSECUTING ATTORNEY:

    Did you know what would happen
    to the people who were selected

ACCUSED #8:

    Mr Prosecutor
    I personally didn't have anything
    against those people

16

There were some like them at home too
Before they were taken away
I always used to tell my family
You go right on buying from them
After all they are human too

PROSECUTING ATTORNEY:

Was that still your attitude
when you were doing platform duty

ACCUSED #8:

Well
except for small troubles
like you get whenever
you have a lot of people in a small place
and except for the gassings
which naturally were terrible
still
everybody had a chance to survive
Personally
I always behaved decently
Anyway what could I do
Orders are orders
And now just because I obeyed
I've got this trial hung on my neck
Mr Prosecutor
I've always tried to live in peace
just like everybody else
and then suddenly I'm hauled out
and everybody starts yelling about Hofmann
That's the one that's Hofmann
they say
What do they want from me

7TH WITNESS:

When we were all lined up
one of the guards came and asked
Does anyone have any physical handicap
A few people stepped forward

They thought
they would get easier work that way
They were sent over to those
who had to go to the left
When the guard led them off
there was a disturbance
and he started shooting
Five or six people were killed

JUDGE:

Does the witness see
the person he has been speaking of
in this room

7TH WITNESS:

Your Honor
it has been many years
since I last stood in front of them
and I find it hard
to look them in the face
That one looks like him
That could be him
His name is Bischof

JUDGE:

Are you sure
or do you have any doubts

7TH WITNESS:

Your Honor
I could not sleep at all last night

COUNSEL FOR THE DEFENSE:

We question the credibility
of the witness
It may be assumed
that he recognized the face of our client
from pictures published in the press
Certainly the exhaustion of the witness
is in itself no proof
of the validity of his testimony

JUDGE:

> Would the accused Bischof
> care to take a stand
> in regard to the accusation

ACCUSED #15:

> I frankly can't understand
> just what the witness is trying to say
> I don't understand either
> why he says
> five or six
> If he had said five
> or if he had said six
> one or the other
> then I could understand it

JUDGE:

> Were you assigned to platform duty

ACCUSED #15:

> All I had to do
> was to organize the prisoners into groups
> I never did any shooting
> Your Honor
> all I would really like to do here
> is make a clean breast of everything
> It has been troubling me deeply for years
> I have developed heart trouble
> from all the worry
> And then they have to foul up
> the last years of my life
> with this whole stinking mess

PROSECUTING ATTORNEY:

> What stinking mess is
> the accused referring to

JUDGE:

> The accused is excited
> Certainly he can scarcely be referring to

the proceedings
initiated by the attorney general
[*The Accused laugh*]
8TH WITNESS:
As a prisoner
I belonged to the clean-up detail
Our job was
to carry off the luggage of the arrivals
The accused Baretzki
took part in the selections on the platform
and he accompanied
the trains to the crematoriums
JUDGE:
Do you recognize the accused
8TH WITNESS:
That is Barrack-leader Baretzki
ACCUSED #13:
I only belonged to the guard unit
For a guard to do the selecting
was out of the question
A barrack-leader could not select the unfit
on his own
Only a doctor could do that
JUDGE:
Were you aware of the purpose
of the selections
ACCUSED #13:
We heard about it
I was deeply shocked
Once when I was home on leave
I told my mother about it
She wouldn't believe it
That's impossible
she said
Anyway people don't burn
because you can't burn flesh

8TH WITNESS:

    I saw
    how Baretzki pointed out the people
    with his swagger stick
    Things never went fast enough for him
    He always tried to speed them up
    Once a train loaded with 3000 people
    came in
    Most of them were sick
    Baretzki yelled at us
    You've got 15 minutes
    to get them out of there
    A baby was born during the unloading
    I wrapped it in a piece of cloth
    and set it down by the mother
    Baretzki came at me with his stick
    and beat me and the woman
    What are you doing with that garbage there
    he yelled
    and he kicked the baby
    so it flew about 10 yards
    Then he ordered
    Bring that shit over here
    By then the child was dead

JUDGE:

    Can you swear to that

8TH WITNESS:

    I can swear to that
    Baretzki had a special way of hitting
    He chopped
    He was known for it

JUDGE:

    What was it like

8TH WITNESS:

    He did it with the flat of his hand
    Like so

Against the aorta
In most cases
it resulted in death
ACCUSED #13:
But the witness just got through saying
that I had a stick
Now if I had a stick
surely
there was no need for me
to hit with my hand
And if I used my hand
then I wouldn't need the stick
Your Honor
the whole thing is a slander
I didn't have any special chop at all
[*The Accused laugh*]

THE SONG OF THE PLATFORM

III

JUDGE:
Who else did you see on the platform
8TH WITNESS:
All the doctors were out on the platform
The selections were part of their work
Dr Frank was there
Dr Schatz and Dr Lucas
COUNSEL FOR THE DEFENSE:
Where were you
while the selections were being made
8TH WITNESS:
At various points on the platform
picking up suitcases
COUNSEL FOR THE DEFENSE:
Can you give us a description
of the platform
8TH WITNESS:
The platform was behind the entrance gates
To the right of the platform
was the men's camp
To the left the women's camp
At the end of the ramp
right and left
the new crematoriums
numbered II and III
At the switch
the trains were usually
shunted onto the track to the right

COUNSEL FOR THE DEFENSE:
    How long was the platform
8TH WITNESS:
    About 850 yards long
COUNSEL FOR THE DEFENSE:
    How long were the trains
8TH WITNESS:
    They usually took up about two thirds
    of the platform
COUNSEL FOR THE DEFENSE:
    Where were the selections carried out
8TH WITNESS:
    In the middle of the platform
COUNSEL FOR THE DEFENSE:
    Where did the people line up
8TH WITNESS:
    At both ends of the platform
COUNSEL FOR THE DEFENSE:
    How wide was the platform
8TH WITNESS:
    About 30 feet wide
COUNSEL FOR THE DEFENSE:
    There the people stood
    in two groups next to each other
    each group lined up in rows of five
    We doubt very much that
    in that crowd
    the witness could have stood
    near the selecting officers
    for any amount of time
JUDGE:
    Accused Dr Frank
    did you take part
    in the selection procedure
ACCUSED #4:
    I was sometimes assigned

24

to platform duty
as a replacement
My assignment was
to remove equipment
from arriving dentists
for use in the camp's dental station
I also registered the dentists
and dental technicians
and saw to it that they were issued clothing
When someone claimed to be a dentist
but in fact wasn't
I did not send him back
After all
we had to have somebody around
to clean up

JUDGE:

Did you ever try
to have yourself released
from platform duty

ACCUSED #4:

I reported to Dr Wirth at headquarters
for that very reason
The only answer given was
Camp duty is front-line duty
Any refusal
will be regarded as desertion
and dealt with accordingly

JUDGE:

Did you escort
transports to the gas chambers

ACCUSED #4:

No
Escort duty was the responsibility
of the guards
I myself did all I could
to help the prisoners

In my ward
I made their stay
as pleasant as possible
They could wear suits that fit
and they didn't have to shave their heads

JUDGE:

Accused Dr Schatz
did you take part in the selections

ACCUSED #5:

I never had anything to do with them
When I was ordered to the platform
to receive medicines
or medical instruments
I did all I could to get out of it
I came to the camp
under protest
I was ordered there
from an infantry dental station
Furthermore I would like to point out
that I enjoyed an unusually cordial
relationship with the prisoners

JUDGE:

Accused Dr Lucas
what did you do on the platform

ACCUSED #6:

I never did anything there at all
Time and again I said
My job as a doctor is to save lives
not destroy them
Also as a Catholic
I cannot take any other position
When attempts were made to force me I said
I was physically unable
I feigned various illnesses and tried
to get transferred back to the army
as soon as possible

I approached my old commanding officer
who said
I should do my best
to avoid making myself
unpleasantly conspicuous
Once on leave I even went so far
as to speak to an archbishop
a friend of mine
and to a prominent lawyer as well
Both told me
that illegal orders need not be obeyed
but that this should not be carried
to the extreme
where one's own life might be endangered
We were at war
and all sorts of things
were going on

PROSECUTING ATTORNEY:

Dr Lucas
what kind of illnesses did you simulate
when you were ordered to take part
in the selections

ACCUSED #6:

I feigned biliary colic
or some kind of stomach upset

PROSECUTING ATTORNEY:

Didn't anyone ever find it odd
that your attacks of colic
occurred only
when you were assigned to platform duty

ACCUSED #6:

There was never any trouble
Passive resistance
was the only way
for me to have as little to do
with those things as possible

I still don't see even now
how else I could have acted then

PROSECUTING ATTORNEY:

And when you did have to participate
what did you do

ACCUSED #6:

Only in three or four cases
my excuses didn't work
I was ordered
to the platform
under the threat
of being taken away then and there
if I did not obey
The meaning of the threat
was unmistakable

PROSECUTING ATTORNEY:

And then you took part in the selections

ACCUSED #6:

All I had to do
was choose people who were fit for work
and the way I chose
many who were obviously unfit
also came into the camp

PROSECUTING ATTORNEY:

And the others

ACCUSED #6:

They were led aside

PROSECUTING ATTORNEY:

When the selection was over
what happened to the luggage

8TH WITNESS:

It was taken to the personal-effects camp
sorted there and stacked

PROSECUTING ATTORNEY:

How large was the personal-effects camp

8TH WITNESS:
    It consisted of 35 barracks
PROSECUTING ATTORNEY:
    Could you estimate
    the amount and value
    of the goods seized
8TH WITNESS:
    Before deportation
    the prisoners had been advised
    to take with them
    as many objects of value as possible
    sheets clothing money and tools
    The reason given was
    that where they were going
    they wouldn't be able to obtain anything
    Thus
    they brought every last thing
    they could
    Much had already been taken from them
    on the platform
    even before the selection began
    The doctors in charge took
    not only medical instruments
    but also suitcases
    full of currency and jewelry
    Then the guards and the trainmen
    took their share
    For us
    too
    there was always something left over
    which we could use to trade with
    later on
    Still when the final inventory
    was drawn up in the personal-effects office
    the total value amounted to millions

PROSECUTING ATTORNEY:
> Could you give us any particulars
> about the value of the goods
> taken from the prisoners

8TH WITNESS:
> According to the final inventory
> covering the period from April 1 1942
> to December 15 1943
> the value of the currency
> stocks precious metals and jewels seized
> amounted to 33 million dollars
> In addition 1900 freight-car loads of textiles
> valued at 12 million dollars
> This does not include the final year
> in which the biggest transports
> were yet to come

PROSECUTING ATTORNEY:
> Who received these assets

8TH WITNESS:
> The goods were forwarded
> to the treasury
> or in some cases to the Department of
> Finance

JUDGE:
> Were there ever any attempts at resistance
> on the platform
> The arrivals greatly outnumbered
> the guards
> They were being separated from their families
> Their possessions were being taken from them
> Did they not resist

9TH WITNESS:
> They did not resist

JUDGE:
> Why not

9TH WITNESS:
> The arrivals were starved
> and exhausted
> Their only desire was
> to rest at last

JUDGE:
> Did they have no idea
> of what was in store for them

9TH WITNESS:
> How could they foresee
> that practically speaking
> they had ceased to exist
> Each one of them still believed
> he could survive

THE SONG OF THE CAMP

I

4TH WITNESS:
   When we had crossed the tracks
   and were lined up
   in front of the camp gate
   I heard
   a prisoner say to one of the women
   That Red Cross truck takes gas
   to the crematoriums
   Your relatives will be killed there
   The woman began to scream
   An officer who had overheard the prisoner
   turned to the woman
   and said
   But my dear woman
   how can you believe
   what a prisoner tells you
   They're all either criminals
   or insane
   Look at the way their ears stick out
   and their shaved heads
   How can you listen to such people
JUDGE:
   Do you recall
   who the officer was
4TH WITNESS:
   I saw him again later
   I was his secretary

in the Political Section
His name is Broad

JUDGE:

Can you point out
the accused Broad

4TH WITNESS:

That is Mr Broad
[*The Accused Broad nods amiably
to the witness*]

JUDGE:

What happened to the prisoner

4TH WITNESS:

I heard
he was sentenced to 150 strokes
for spreading reports of atrocities
He died from it

JUDGE:

Does the accused Broad
have anything to say to this

ACCUSED #16:

I don't recall the case
But 150 strokes
We never ordered that many

3RD WITNESS:

Even though our luggage was left behind
and we were separated
from our families
we still walked unsuspecting
through the gate between the barbed wire
We thought
our wives and children
were going to be fed on the other side
and that we would be allowed
to see them again soon
But then we saw

hundreds of ragged figures
many of them starved down to skeletons
We lost all hope

6TH WITNESS:

One of them came up to us
and shouted
Prisoners
See that smoke behind the barracks
That smoke
is your wives and children
And for you too now that you're in here
there's only one way out
Up through the soot in the chimneys

3RD WITNESS:

We were pushed into a washroom barrack
Guards and prisoners came
with stacks of papers
We had to strip
and everything we still had on us
was taken away
Watches rings papers pictures
were registered in personal files
Then numbers were tattooed
on the left forearm

JUDGE:

How was this done

3RD WITNESS:

The numbers were pricked into our skin
with a needle stamp
then ink was rubbed in
Our hair was cut off
and we had a cold shower
After that we got our clothes

JUDGE:

What clothes were you given

34

3RD WITNESS:
> A pair of shorts full of holes
> an undershirt
> a torn jacket
> a pair of patched pants
> a cap
> and a pair of wooden shoes
> Then we set off at the double
> to our barrack

JUDGE:
> What did your barrack look like

3RD WITNESS:
> A wooden barrack without windows
> A door in the front and one in the back
> Small skylights up under the roof
> Right and left
> three-decker bunks
> the bottom level on the ground
> the bunks supported by partition beams
> Length of the barrack about 130 feet

JUDGE:
> How many prisoners
> were quartered there

3RD WITNESS:
> It was built to hold 500 people
> There were 1000 of us

JUDGE:
> How many such barracks were there

3RD WITNESS:
> More than 200

JUDGE:
> How wide were the bunks

3RD WITNESS:
> About six feet
> Six men to a bunk

They had to keep shifting from
their right side over to their left
JUDGE:
  Was any bedding provided
3RD WITNESS:
  Some of the bunks had straw
  The straw was rotten
  and it sifted down from the top
  onto the lower bunks
  There was one blanket for each bunk
  The men who lay on the outside
  kept trying to pull the blanket
  over their way
  The strongest lay in the middle
JUDGE:
  Were the barracks heated
3RD WITNESS:
  There were two stoves
  The stovepipes went into a chimney
  in the middle of the barrack
  They were bricked over
  and the top of the brickwork
  served as a table
  The stoves were hardly ever heated
JUDGE:
  Were there sanitary installations
  in the barracks
3RD WITNESS:
  There were wood troughs for washing
  in the washroom barracks
  A pipe with holes in it ran over the troughs
  Water dripped out of the pipe
  In the latrine there were long cement troughs
  covered with boards with round holes in them
  200 people could use them at one time

The latrine detail saw to it
that nobody sat there too long
They clubbed the prisoners right and left
to drive them out
Many of the prisoners
simply couldn't get done that quick
Part of their rectum stuck out from the strain
As soon as they had been driven out
of the latrine
they got back in line
There wasn't any paper
Many people tore pieces off their clothes
to wipe themselves with
or stole
pieces from each other's clothes at night
to have some in reserve
You had to relieve yourself in the morning
After that you couldn't
Anybody caught trying
was locked up
Water from the washroom barracks drained
into the latrine
to carry off the filth on the floor
The latrines kept getting stopped up
because the water pressure was too low
Then the shit detail came in
to pump it out
The stink from the latrines
mixed in with the smell
of the smoke

4TH WITNESS:

The bowls we were given
served three different functions
to wash in
to get our supper in

and to relieve ourselves in at night
In the women's camp
the only place you could get water
was right next to the latrine
At that thin trickle of water
that ran off into the vats full of excrement
women stood and drank
and tried
to collect enough water in their bowls
so they could wash
Those who gave up washing
had given up

5TH WITNESS:

Even as I jumped out of the freight car
into that confusion on the platform
I knew that what mattered here was
to look out for yourself
to try to work your way up
to make a good impression
and to keep away from anything
that might drag you down
When they made us lie down on the tables
in the reception room
and inspected our rectums
and our sexual organs
for concealed valuables
every last remnant
of our usual life
vanished
Family
home
occupation
and possessions
were ideas
that were wiped out

when the number
was stamped into your arm
And already we had started to live
with a new set of values
and to adjust to this world
which for anyone
who wanted to survive in it
became a normal world
The supreme commandment was
to stay healthy
and to show you were physically strong
I stuck close to those
who were too weak
to eat their rations
so I could take their food
at the first opportunity
I didn't take my eyes off
those who were dying
if they had a better sleeping place than I
Our way up in this new society
started in the barrack
which was our home now
From starting out sleeping
on the cold mud floor
we fought our way up
to the warm places on the top bunks
When two had to eat
out of the same bowl
they stared at each other's throats
to make sure
the other wasn't swallowing
an extra spoonful
It was normal
that everything had been stolen from us
It was normal

that we stole too
Dirt sores and diseases
were what was normal
It was normal
that all around us people were dying
and it was normal
to live in the face of one's own death
Our feelings grew numb
and we looked at corpses
with complete indifference
and that was normal
And it was normal
that there were some among us
who helped those who stood over us
to beat us
The woman who became
the Barrack-elder's maid
had come up in that world
and those who managed
to ingratiate themselves
with the Barrack-leader
rose even higher
Only the cunning survived
only those who every day
with unrelenting alertness
took and held their bit of ground
The unfit
the retarded
the slow
the gentle
the bewildered and the impractical
the ones who mourned and the ones
who pitied themselves
were crushed
6TH WITNESS:
The first morning

we lined up for roll call
It was raining
We stood there for hours
Behind the barbed wire
on the other side of the platform
the women were beating beaten
and shoved into trucks
They were naked and they screamed
at us
They wanted us to help them
and we couldn't help them

4TH WITNESS:

I walked into a barrack
that was full of corpses
I saw
something move a little among the dead
It was a young girl
I pulled her out of the barrack
into the street
and asked
Who are you
How long have you been here
I don't know
she said
Why were you lying in there
with the dead
I asked
I can't be with the living any more
she said
She died that night

5TH WITNESS:

We were sent out to dig graves
Many of the women collapsed
trying to shovel the mud out
We were up to our hips in water
The guards stood by looking on

They were very young
One of the women turned to the captain
Captain
she said
I can't work this hard any more
I'm pregnant
The guards laughed
and one of them pushed her
down with a shovel
and kept her under the water
until she drowned

7TH WITNESS:

I heard
a guard talking through the barbed wire
to a nine-year-old boy
You know a lot for a boy your age
he said
The boy answered
I know that I know a lot
and I also know
I'm not going to learn any more
He was loaded into a truck
with a group
of about 90 children
When the children started
screaming and struggling
the boy yelled
Get in here
Get in the truck
Stop your crying
You saw the way
your parents and grandparents
went
Climb in
then you'll get to see them again
And as they were being driven off

I heard
him shout back to the guard
You won't be forgiven
anything

THE SONG OF THE CAMP

II

8TH WITNESS:
    In the morning we got
    a pint of coffee substitute
    and a fifth of an ounce of sugar
    Some of us
    still had a piece of dry bread
    saved up from the night before
    At noon we got soup
    It was made out of scraps of potatoes
    turnips and cabbage
    a minimum of meat or fat
    and a mealy nutrient
    that gave the soup
    its typical taste
    Sometimes there were pieces of paper
    or rags in the soup
    Prisoners fought
    to get not to the head of the line
    but as near the end as they could
    The top third of the soup
    was water
    Only toward the bottom
    was there anything nourishing
    In the evening after roll call
    each of us got his piece of bread
    from 10 to 12 ounces
    and various supplements
    about ¾ of an ounce of sausage

an ounce of margarine
or a teaspoonful of turnip jelly
On Friday we sometimes got
five or six potatoes
Often these extra rations
were cut in half
or weren't given out at all
because the camp personnel
from the guards on
up to the commanding officer
helped themselves
to the prisoners' food supply store
as much as they wanted

PROSECUTING ATTORNEY:

How many calories
did the daily rations contain

8TH WITNESS:

About 1000 to 1300 calories
At rest
the body uses 1700
At hard labor
it requires about 4800
Since all the prisoners worked hard
their last reserves were quickly consumed
Movements grew progressively slower
according to the various stages of hunger
until there was no strength left
to keep the body in motion
Drowsiness and apathy
were characteristic symptoms
of weakness
Emaciation of the body
was accompanied by an exhaustion of mind
which terminated in a complete loss
of interest in all external events
In this condition

a prisoner could no longer
concentrate his thoughts
His memory was so greatly weakened
that frequently he could not
even remember his own name
On the average
a prisoner could not hold out
longer than three months

COUNSEL FOR THE DEFENSE:

How then did you
manage to survive

8TH WITNESS:

Those who survived
were only those
who in the first few weeks managed
to get some kind of inside position
either because of their specialized skills
or by being assigned to special duties
in the camp work
A special-duty prisoner
who knew how to
exploit the privileges of his position
could obtain practically anything

COUNSEL FOR THE DEFENSE:

What privileged position did you hold

8TH WITNESS:

I was a prisoner doctor
At first in the quarantine camp
Later in the infirmary

JUDGE:

What were the conditions there

8TH WITNESS:

In the quarantine camp there were rats
They bit not only the corpses
but also the critically ill
In the morning the feet of the dying

were often bleeding from rat bites
At night the rats took the bread
out of the prisoners' pockets
The prisoners frequently accused each other
You stole my bread
But it was the rats
Fleas infested the camp
by the million
Those who had boots got rid of them
because the fleas
made those precious possessions unbearable
With socks and rags
you could at least scratch
Conditions in the prisoners' infirmary
were better
There were crepe-paper bandages
cellulose
a keg of ichthyol ointment
and a barrel of talcum powder
All wounds were treated with the ointment
and barber's itch was covered with talcum
so it wouldn't show
We had a few tablets of aspirin
They were strung up on thread
Patients with fever under 100 degrees
were allowed one lick
Patients with fever over 100 degrees
could lick twice

JUDGE:
What were the most common illnesses
8TH WITNESS:
Aside from general weakness
and bodily injuries caused by ill-treatment
we had spotted fever and paratyphoid fever
abdominal typhus erysipelas and tuberculosis
as well as the characteristic camp disease

incurable diarrhea
Furunculosis flourished in the camp
Guards clubbed abscesses open
until the skin peeled off to the bone
In the camp I saw diseases
I never dreamed I would see
diseases
one only reads about in medical texts
There was Noma for instance
a disease that occurs
only in completely debilitated people
eating holes through the cheeks
until you can see
right through to the teeth
Or phemphicus
an extremely rare disease
which detaches the skin
in blisters
and after a few days
results in death

9TH WITNESS:

After the evening roll call
the Barrack-elder
picked some of us out for exercise
We had to hop like frogs
He kept shouting
Jump faster faster
and if somebody didn't keep up
he pounded them with a footstool
until they collapsed

JUDGE:

What was this Barrack-elder's name

9TH WITNESS:

His name was Bednarek
I can point him out

ACCUSED #18:

I never heard of anybody being beaten
during the exercise period

JUDGE:

What did take place
during the exercise period

ACCUSED #18:

Prisoners who attracted attention
had to do some light exercises
To the left
To the right
That was all

9TH WITNESS:

In winter Bednarek made
prisoners stand under the cold shower
for half an hour
until they were numb with cold
Then they were thrown out into the yard
where they died

ACCUSED #18:

These accusations are simply made up
I couldn't possibly
have done that sort of thing
I was a special-duty prisoner myself
I had the Kapo over me
the work supervisor
and the camp-elder
I myself
and I can say it with pride today
let prisoners sleep in my room
and in our block after supper
we always had a good time

9TH WITNESS:

After Bednarek
had beaten a prisoner to death

he went into his room
and prayed

ACCUSED #18:

It's true
I'm a religious man
But as for praying I didn't dare
There were too many informers for that
And I never killed anybody
At the most
there was maybe a slap now and then
when I had to break up an argument

3RD WITNESS:

More than any of the others
there was one who was first
when it came to beating or killing
His name was Kaduk
Kaduk we all knew what that name meant

JUDGE:

Could the witness
point out the accused Kaduk

3RD WITNESS:

That is Mr Kaduk
      [*The Accused grins at the witness*]
The prisoners called him
Professor
or
the Holy Doctor Kaduk
because he carried out
selections on his own
With the crook of his walking stick
he fished out his victims
by the neck or leg

ACCUSED #7:

Mr Chairman
that statement is not true

3RD WITNESS:

> I was there
> when Kaduk had hundreds of prisoners
> hauled out of the hospital
> They had to strip in the laundry barrack
> and then run past Kaduk
> in single file
> He held his walking stick out
> about a yard off the ground
> in front of him
> They had to jump over it
> If they touched the stick
> they were taken off to be gassed
> If they cleared it without touching it
> they were beaten until they collapsed
> Now try it again
> Kaduk shouted
> But the second time
> nobody cleared it

ACCUSED #7:

> I selected no prisoners
> I made no decisions
> I had no such authority

JUDGE:

> What was within your authority

ACCUSED #7:

> I had to be on hand
> during the selections
> I watched like a hawk
> to make sure nobody
> from the selected group slipped over
> into the work-fit group

JUDGE:

> Did you have any other duties
> on the platform

ACCUSED #7:
>   Yes
>   I had to organize
>   the group traffic

JUDGE:
>   How did you do that

ACCUSED #7:
>   Everybody out
>   Baggage on the platform
>   Fall in columns of five
>   Forward march

3RD WITNESS:
>   Kaduk fired
>   at random
>   into the crowd

ACCUSED #7:
>   I never even thought of
>   firing at random
>   If I had wanted to shoot
>   I would have hit
>   whoever I was aiming at
>   I was strict
>   I'll admit that
>   But I only did
>   what I had to do

JUDGE:
>   And what did you have to do

ACCUSED #7:
>   Make sure that the operation ran smoothly
>   It was regulations that children
>   were immediately set aside
>   also mothers who didn't want
>   to be separated from their children
>   Everything went without a hitch
>   The transports rolled in
>   like a line of sausages

There wasn't any need to rough anybody up
They all took it very well
They didn't resist
since they could see
resistance would have been pointless

6TH WITNESS:

Once Kaduk hit one of the prisoners
in our work detail
knocked him down
then laid his walking stick
down across his throat
put one foot on each end of the stick
and rocked from side to side
until the man choked to death

ACCUSED #7:

Lies
Lies

JUDGE:

Sit down Kaduk
You will not shout at the witness

ACCUSED #7:

Mr Chairman
What he says there
simply isn't true
All I care about here is the truth
No prisoner was ever killed
that way in our camp
We had orders
to go easy
with the work force
Sometimes though I'd only lift my hand
and somebody would fall over
pretending he had fainted

    [*The Accused laugh*]

Mr Chairman
we weren't interested in beating anybody

We were on our feet
from 5:30 in the morning
and then at night we
still had to go on platform duty
That was enough for us
Mr Chairman
all I want is to live in peace
These last years have proved that
I was a hospital attendant
and my patients loved me
They can bear me out on that
Papa Kaduk
that's what they called me
Doesn't that tell the whole story
Why should I have to pay now
for what I had to do then
Everybody else did it too
So why of all people
did they arrest me

THE SONG OF THE CAMP

III

4TH WITNESS:
The more you managed to push down
whoever was under you
the more secure your own position was
I could see the whole face
of our Barrack-elder change
when she talked to a superior
She was cheerful and friendly then
and behind that you could feel her fear
Sometimes her supervisor
treated her like her best friend
and she enjoyed many privileges
But if the supervisor
had had a bad night just once
then she would be done for
from one minute to the next
And she had already been through everything
she had seen her relatives shot down
she had been forced to watch
as they murdered her children
she had grown completely numb
like the rest of us
She knew
that once she went under
nobody would help her
and whoever took over
would go on beating
so she beat us

because she wanted
to stay on top at any price
5TH WITNESS:
The question
of right and wrong
didn't exist any longer
The only thing that counted
was what was immediately useful
Only our masters could afford
to have moods
and even to show how moved they were
or to be sympathetic
and make plans for the future
The camp doctor Dr Rohde
let me work in his ward
He found out
we had gone to school in the same city
and asked me
if we hadn't perhaps met each other
at the Ritter
where he frequently stopped in
for a glass of wine
and I thought
Fine if that's the way you want it
I'll go along with you
and so I reminded him of his youth
and he said
After the war we'll meet there again
for a glass of wine
Dr Mengele sent flowers to a pregnant
  woman
and the wife of the camp commander
sent her best regards
and a baby sweater she had knitted herself
to the children's barrack
where somebody had thought

it would be a nice idea
to paint dwarfs on the walls
and set up a sandbox
The paths to the crematoriums
were carefully raked after each batch
of prisoners had gone by
The bushes along the way were trimmed
and flower beds had been planted
in the grass that grew
over the underground chambers
Mengele used to arrive smartly dressed
his thumbs stuck in his belt
He would nod pleasantly to the children
who called him Uncle
before they were cut up in his laboratory
But there was another man I remember
His name was Flacke
Nobody starved to death in his ward
and the prisoners there all wore
clean clothes
I asked him once
Sir who are you doing this for
Someday
we will all have to be done away with
because not a single witness
can be left behind
He said
There will be enough of us here
who will find a way to prevent that
PROSECUTING ATTORNEY:
Do you mean to say
that each one of the men in charge
could take a stand
against conditions in the camp
and change them

5TH WITNESS:
>   That is exactly what I was trying to say
1ST WITNESS:
>   Normal reactions
>   were possible only in the first few hours
>   After one had been there for a time
>   it was impossible
>   Once you fell into the routine
>   you were caught
>   and had to cooperate
PROSECUTING ATTORNEY:
>   As a doctor
>   you were assigned to prevent
>   the spread of epidemics
1ST WITNESS:
>   Cases of spotted and typhoid fever
>   had broken out among some
>   of the camp personnel and their families
>   I was ordered
>   by the Health Institute
>   to report to the camp
PROSECUTING ATTORNEY:
>   Then your presence there had nothing to do
>   with treating the prisoners themselves
1ST WITNESS:
>   No
PROSECUTING ATTORNEY:
>   Did you get an impression
>   of conditions in the camp
1ST WITNESS:
>   Shortly after I arrived
>   the doctor in charge of the laboratory said
>   I realize this is all new to you
>   but it's not half so bad
>   We don't have anything to do
>   with the liquidation program here

and it's none of our business either
If after two weeks
you decide you don't want to stay here
you can leave
With the intention to leave the camp
after two weeks
I went to work
A few days later
the chief camp doctor Dr Wirth
ordered me to take part
in the selections on the platform
When I told him
I don't want to have anything to do
with that
he said
You won't have much to do there
But I still refused

PROSECUTING ATTORNEY:
What happened when you refused

1ST WITNESS:
Nothing
I didn't have to take part
in the selections

PROSECUTING ATTORNEY:
Did you leave the camp
after your first two weeks

1ST WITNESS:
No
I decided to stay after all
and see if I couldn't do something
about the contagious diseases
I felt that I could
at least in a few cases
prevent things
without exposing myself

As a result of my work the threat
of the epidemic was ended

PROSECUTING ATTORNEY:

Among the camp personnel that is
Not among the prisoners

1ST WITNESS:

Yes
That was my assignment

JUDGE:

You were at that time in charge
of the sentry units both within
and outside the camp
also of the guard units
attached to the work details
What did that involve

2ND WITNESS:

My assignment was
to keep an eye on the guards
to see they carried out their charge
diligently and faithfully

JUDGE:

What regulations were they under

2ND WITNESS:

When a prisoner tried to escape
the guard was required to call out three times
before firing a warning shot
If the prisoner still didn't halt
he was to be shot
to prevent further flight

JUDGE:

Were any prisoners shot
for this reason

2ND WITNESS:

Not under my command

JUDGE:

Did prisoners

run up against the electrically charged
barbed wires

2ND WITNESS:

Not under my command

JUDGE:

Did it ever occur

2ND WITNESS:

I heard it happened sometimes

JUDGE:

Did guard details
obey regulations

2ND WITNESS:

As far as I know
Yes
On my word of honor

JUDGE:

Do you know anything about cap shooting

2ND WITNESS:

About what

JUDGE:

Shooting caps

2ND WITNESS:

I've heard about it

JUDGE:

What did you hear

2ND WITNESS:

They said
caps were thrown up
and then they shot at them

JUDGE:

Who threw the caps
whose caps
and who did the shooting

2ND WITNESS:

That I don't know

JUDGE:

What were you told then

2ND WITNESS:

Yes

Well

A prisoner was ordered

to take off his cap

and throw it away

and then

Move

run and get your cap they'd say

and when he started to run

they'd shoot him down

JUDGE:

And if he didn't run

2ND WITNESS:

Then they'd shoot him too

because that was refusal to obey an order

PROSECUTING ATTORNEY:

Were special rations

or special leaves granted

as a reward for

shooting prisoners attempting escape

2ND WITNESS:

I never heard of that happening

I don't believe it either

To be rewarded for such behavior

would degrade a soldier's reputation

PROSECUTING ATTORNEY:

The court has in its possession

documents which show

that in a number of instances

sentries were rewarded for

shooting prisoners attempting escape

Furthermore lists of prisoners

shot while attempting escape

were posted and periodically
brought up to date

2ND WITNESS:
That's news to me

PROSECUTING ATTORNEY:
According to our information
you are currently
director of an insurance company

COUNSEL FOR THE DEFENSE:
We object to
these irrelevant interjections
by the prosecution

PROSECUTING ATTORNEY:
We take it for granted
that the witness
realizes the significance
of a signature

2ND WITNESS:
Certainly

PROSECUTING ATTORNEY:
Some of these lists
bear your signature

2ND WITNESS:
It's possible
that on some occasion
I had to sign as a matter of routine
I can't remember

THE SONG OF THE SWING

I

JUDGE:
   As a prisoner
   you were employed
   in the Political Division
   What did you do there
5TH WITNESS:
   At first I was stenographer and typist
   in the administrative office
   then because of my knowledge of languages
   I was made interpreter
JUDGE:
   Who assigned you to this position
5TH WITNESS:
   Mr Boger
JUDGE:
   Do you recognize
   Boger among the accused
5TH WITNESS:
   That is Mr Boger
      [*The accused Boger
      greets the witness amiably*]
COUNSEL FOR THE DEFENSE:
   Where precisely
   was the Political Division located
5TH WITNESS:
   It was a wooden barrack
   directly behind the entrance

COUNSEL FOR THE DEFENSE:
    Behind which entrance
5TH WITNESS:
    Just to the left behind the entrance
    to the old camp
COUNSEL FOR THE DEFENSE:
    How far was the old camp
    from the main camp
5TH WITNESS:
    About two miles
COUNSEL FOR THE DEFENSE:
    Where were your living quarters
5TH WITNESS:
    In the women's camp
COUNSEL FOR THE DEFENSE:
    Could you describe for us
    the way you took to your office
5TH WITNESS:
    We had to leave camp
    every morning
    and walk along the side of the fields
    The road crossed the tracks
    where the switch engines
    shunted the freight cars
    We frequently had to wait at the barrier
    On the other side of the tracks
    there were more fields
    and a couple of empty farmhouses
    Then we went through a barred gate
    There were trees
    and the old crematorium
    Next to it was the Political Division
COUNSEL FOR THE DEFENSE:
    Was the Political Division
    within the camp proper

5TH WITNESS:

It was outside the camp
First
there were the administration buildings
Then the two barbed-wire fences
and the observation towers
Behind that were the barracks
where the prisoners lived

COUNSEL FOR THE DEFENSE:

What did the Political Division barrack
look like

5TH WITNESS:

It was one story high
and painted green

COUNSEL FOR THE DEFENSE:

What did the administrative office look like

5TH WITNESS:

There were flower pots on the window sills
and there were curtains
and on the walls
pictures and mottoes

COUNSEL FOR THE DEFENSE:

What kind of pictures and mottoes

5TH WITNESS:

I can't remember any more

COUNSEL FOR THE DEFENSE:

Who supervised the work in the office

5TH WITNESS:

Mr Broad
We typists always had
to look our best
We were allowed to let our hair grow
We wore kerchiefs
and civilian clothes and shoes
We spat on our shoes in the morning
and polished them with our hands

COUNSEL FOR THE DEFENSE:

How did Mr Boger treat you

5TH WITNESS:

Mr Boger always treated me decently
Frequently he gave me his mess kit
with the leftovers
He saved my life once
when I was about to be transferred
to a penal company
A Kapo had reported me
for doing a careless job of dusting
Mr Boger revoked the sentence

JUDGE:

How many typists worked
in the Political Division

5TH WITNESS:

We were 16 girls

JUDGE:

What did you have to do

5TH WITNESS:

We had to keep the death lists up to date
We had to enter the particulars
relating to date and cause of death
This was called the Discharge
Mr Broad grew furious
if he found a single mistake in our typing

JUDGE:

How was the filing organized

5TH WITNESS:

There were two tables
On one table
were the card-index boxes
with the numbers of the living
On the other the boxes
with the numbers of the dead·
By looking at these we could see

how many from a given shipment
were still alive
Out of a hundred after a week
there were two dozen

JUDGE:

Were all deaths
that occurred within the camp
recorded there

5TH WITNESS:

Only prisoners
who had received a number
were kept on the books
Those who were taken directly
from the platform to the gas
were not entered on any list

JUDGE:

What were the causes of death
that you entered

5TH WITNESS:

Most of them
were fictitious
For instance we were not allowed to write
Shot while attempting escape
but had to write heart attack instead
Instead of malnutrition we wrote
dysentery
We had to make sure
no two prisoners died at the same minute
and that the cause of death
corresponded to their age
Therefore no 20-year-old could die
of a weak heart
In the beginning letters were still sent
to the next of kin

PROSECUTING ATTORNEY:

Can you recall the text of these letters

5TH WITNESS:

    In spite of all medical treatment
    it has unfortunately been impossible
    to save the life of the detained
    We extend our deepest sympathies
    to you for this great loss
    At your request the urn
    will be sent to you
    COD at a cost of three dollars

PROSECUTING ATTORNEY:

    Were the ashes of the deceased
    actually in these urns

5TH WITNESS:

    The ashes of many dead
    were in those urns
    We could see out of the windows
    the dead piled up
    in front of the old crematorium
    They were dumped there by the truckload

PROSECUTING ATTORNEY:

    Could you give us an idea
    of the number of the dead
    entered in your office

5TH WITNESS:

    We worked 12 to 15 hours a day
    on the official books of the dead
    It came to about 300 dead per day

PROSECUTING ATTORNEY:

    Were any of those deaths
    caused directly
    by the Political Division

5TH WITNESS:

    Prisoners died there daily
    either by mistreatment or execution

COUNSEL FOR THE DEFENSE:

    Where were the prisoners executed

5TH WITNESS:

In the camp in Barrack 11

COUNSEL FOR THE DEFENSE:

Were you allowed to enter the camp

5TH WITNESS:

No
but we knew of everything that went on
Every memorandum and report
related to the camp
passed through our office
Boger said to us
What you hear and see here
you have neither heard nor seen

JUDGE:

How were the interrogations
in the Political Division carried out

5TH WITNESS:

Boger always began very calmly
He came up close to the prisoner
and asked the questions
that I had to interpret
If the prisoner didn't answer
he shook a bunch of keys
in front of the man's face
If the prisoner still didn't answer
Boger hit him in the face with the keys
Then he went up even closer
and said
I have a machine
that will make you talk

JUDGE:

What sort of machine was this

5TH WITNESS:

Boger called it his talking machine

JUDGE:

Where was it

5TH WITNESS:
In the next room
JUDGE:
Did you ever see the machine
5TH WITNESS:
Yes
JUDGE:
What did it look like
5TH WITNESS:
It was made out of poles
COUNSEL FOR THE DEFENSE:
Are you sure
you remember this correctly
5TH WITNESS:
It was a frame
They were hung on it
We heard the beating and the screaming
After an hour
or after several hours
they were carried out
They were unrecognizable
JUDGE:
Were they still alive
5TH WITNESS:
If they weren't dead then
they seldom lived much longer
Once Boger saw me crying
He said
This is no place for personal feelings
JUDGE:
For what reasons were prisoners
subjected to such punishment
5TH WITNESS:
Sometimes it was because somebody
had stolen a piece of bread
or because he was too slow

in responding to an order to work faster
Frequently it was enough that an informer
had denounced somebody
There was an informer's box
Anybody could drop a note in

ACCUSED #2:

I had nothing to do
with that kind of nonsense
In the Political Division we dealt
exclusively with resistance problems
within the camp

JUDGE:

How often did the witness herself see
prisoners die
after being taken down from the machine

5TH WITNESS:

At least 20 times

JUDGE:

You can vouch for the fact
that in at least 20 cases
prisoners died in your presence

5TH WITNESS:

Yes

JUDGE:

Did you ever see
the punishment being carried out

5TH WITNESS:

Yes
I saw a man hanging there once
with his head down
Another time a woman was
strapped up on the poles
Boger forced us
to go in and look

ACCUSED #2:

It is true

that the witness was an interpreter
However she was never present
at any of the intensive interrogations
On such occasions
ladies were never permitted

5TH WITNESS:

Ladies

ACCUSED #2:

I think I can say that now
[*The Accused laugh*]

JUDGE:

Did the witness
see any of the accused present
take part in the beatings

5TH WITNESS:

I saw Boger in his shirt sleeves
holding his whip
and I often saw him
come out spattered with blood
Once I heard Broad say to Lachmann
another member of the Political Division
You know Gerhard
he spouted blood like a pig
Then he handed me his coat
to clean
They always made a big point
of cleanliness
Broad liked to look at himself in the mirror
looking very pleased
especially after he was promoted
to private first class
and I had sewed
his stripe on for him
I had to clean Boger's boots once

JUDGE:

Yes

5TH WITNESS:

    A truckload of children
    drove by outside
    I saw it through the office window
    A small boy jumped off the truck
    He was holding an apple
    Boger came out the door
    The child stood there with his apple
    Boger went over to the child
    grabbed him by the ankles
    and smashed his head
    against the barrack wall
    Then he picked up the apple
    called me out and said
    Wipe that off the wall
    Later at an interrogation
    I saw him eat the apple

COUNSEL FOR THE DEFENSE:

    You made no mention of this
    at the preliminary hearings

5TH WITNESS:

    I couldn't speak about it

COUNSEL FOR THE DEFENSE:

    Why not

5TH WITNESS:

    For personal reasons

COUNSEL FOR THE DEFENSE:

    Could you tell us
    what those reasons are

5TH WITNESS:

    Since that time
    I have never wanted to have
    a child of my own

COUNSEL FOR THE DEFENSE:

    How is it
    that you can speak about it now

5TH WITNESS:

Now that I see him again
I must speak

JUDGE:

What does the accused Boger
have to say in reply
to these accusations

ACCUSED #2:

They are completely made up
a poor way for the witness to repay me
for the trust
I placed in her in those days

THE SONG OF THE SWING

II

7TH WITNESS:
    I was brought into the interrogation room
    of the Political Division
    together with some other prisoners
JUDGE:
    Can you describe this room
7TH WITNESS:
    There were expensive rugs on the floor
    that had come off
    one of the transports from France
    Boger's desk
    was set at an angle across from the door
    He was sitting on the desk when I came in
    The interpreter sat behind the desk
JUDGE:
    Who else was present in the room
7TH WITNESS:
    The head of the Political Division
    Grabner
    and the accused Dylewski and Broad
JUDGE:
    What did they say
7TH WITNESS:
    Boger said
    We are the Political Division
    We don't ask questions
    We listen
    You ought to know what you have to say

JUDGE:
    Why had you been brought there
7TH WITNESS:
    I didn't know
    I didn't know what
    I was supposed to say
    and I asked them to question me
    I was beaten senseless
    When I came to I was lying in the hall
    Boger was standing there
    He said
    Get up
    But I couldn't get up
    He came toward me
    I pulled myself up against the wall
    I saw I was bleeding
    The floor and my clothes
    were covered with blood
    My head was split open
    My nose was broken
    All that afternoon and most of the night
    I had to stand with my face to the wall
    There were several others standing there
    Anybody who turned
    had his head knocked against the wall
    The next day I was interrogated again
    I was brought into the room
    with the other prisoners
JUDGE:
    What did they want to find out
7TH WITNESS:
    The whole time I didn't know
    what it was all about
    A couple of times they
    put something around my head
    some kind of metal band I think

Then I was taken back to the hall
and Boger took the man next to me
into the room
His name was Walter Windmuller
JUDGE:
Do you know what happened to him
7TH WITNESS:
He was in there for about
two or three hours
I stood in the hallway
with my face to the wall
Then Windmuller came out
He had to stand next to me
Blood was running down his legs
He fell over several times
We had learned
how to talk without moving our lips
When I asked him what had happened
he said
They smashed my balls in there
He died the same day
JUDGE:
Was Boger responsible
for this prisoner's death
7TH WITNESS:
I am convinced that
if Boger didn't do the killing himself
he certainly helped kill him
JUDGE:
Does the accused Boger
have anything to say
ACCUSED #2:
Mr Chairman
if I may be allowed to explain
that's not the way it happened

JUDGE:

How did it happen

ACCUSED #2:

Mr Chairman

I didn't kill anybody

I just had to carry out my interrogations

JUDGE:

What kind of interrogations were they

ACCUSED #2:

Occasionally

they were intensive interrogations

conducted

according to standard operating procedures

JUDGE:

What was the reason for these procedures

ACCUSED #2:

In the interest of camp security

it was essential

to take vigorous measures

against traitors and other harmful elements

JUDGE:

Accused Boger

as a criminal investigator

didn't you know

that a man

subjected to such an interrogation

will say anything you want him to say

ACCUSED #2:

That's not the way I see it at all

and especially not in view of

our specific task

If a prisoner proved stubborn

force was the only way

to make him confess

8TH WITNESS:

When I was called into Boger's room

I saw
a plateful of herrings on his desk
Grabner asked me if I was hungry
I said no
But Grabner said
I know how long it's been
since you've eaten
Today you're going to see
how nice I can be
I'm going to give you something to eat
Boger's made a salad for you
He ordered me to eat
I couldn't
because my hands were handcuffed
behind my back
Then Boger pushed my face into the plate
I had to eat the herrings
They were so salty that I threw up
I had to lick up
the vomit together with the herrings
I still had some in my mouth
and Boger shouted
Watch him to make sure he doesn't
spit any of it out in the hall
Then they took me to Barrack 11
and up to the loft
My hands were tied behind me
I was hung from a pole by my hands
That was called pole-hanging
They hung you up just high enough
so that the bottom of your feet
barely touched the floor
Boger pushed me back and forth
and kicked me in the stomach
There was a pail of water in front of me
Boger asked me if I wanted to drink

He laughed and twisted me
one way and then the other
When I lost consciousness
they threw water over me
My arms grew numb
My wrists almost snapped
Boger questioned me
but my tongue was so swollen
I couldn't speak
Then Boger said
We still have another swing for you
I was
taken back to the Political Division

COUNSEL FOR THE DEFENSE:
Were you subjected to a session
on that swing too

8TH WITNESS:
Yes

COUNSEL FOR THE DEFENSE:
Then it was possible
to survive it after all

THE SONG OF THE SWING

III

8TH WITNESS:
>I remember one morning
>in the spring of 1942
>A platoon of prisoner police
>marched up in front of the barrack
>of the former post office
>where the Political Division
>had been installed
>At the head of the column were prisoners
>carrying two wooden supports
>built like the sides of a hurdle
>Behind them were guards
>armed with submachine guns
>and behind them
>the heads of the Political Division
>They had their briefcases
>and especially prepared dried-out bullwhips
>that they used for corporal punishment
>Those supports
>were the frame for the new swing

JUDGE:
>Was that the first time
>the apparatus was used

8TH WITNESS:
>It had existed before
>in a simpler form
>At first it was just a pipe
>laid across two tables

and the prisoner was strapped to the pipe
Since the pipe turned when the prisoner
was beaten
this new frame was made to keep it stable

COUNSEL FOR THE DEFENSE:

Would the witness
tell us how he happens to know this

8TH WITNESS:

Nothing happened in our part of the camp
that we didn't know about
In the old camp everything took place
at close quarters
The whole camp wasn't more than
about 200 yards wide and 300 long
From any one of the 28 barracks
you could see the whole camp

JUDGE:

What was the reason for your being
brought in for interrogation

8TH WITNESS:

I was assigned to the work detail
that put in the drainage ditch
around the outside of the camp
On the job I helped a fellow prisoner
get together with his mother
who was in the women's camp
The prisoner's name was Janicki
They took him
into the interrogation room first
When they were done with him
they threw him out into the hall
He was still alive
He opened his mouth
and stuck out his tongue as far as he could
He started to lick the floor
he was so thirsty

Boger came up and turned his head
with the toe of his boot
Then he said
It's your turn now
If you don't tell us the truth
the same thing will happen to you
Then they strapped me up on the swing

JUDGE:

Would you
describe the procedure

8TH WITNESS:

First the prisoner had
to sit down on the floor
and draw up his knees
His hands were tied in front
and then pushed down over his knees
Then they shoved the pipe in the space
between the arms and knees
Then the pipe was raised
and set into the wood frame

JUDGE:

Who took care of these preparations

8TH WITNESS:

Two special-duty prisoners

JUDGE:

Who else was in the room

8TH WITNESS:

I saw Boger there
and Broad and Dylewski
Boger asked the questions
but I couldn't answer
I hung with my head down
and the two special-duty prisoners
swung me back and forth

COUNSEL FOR THE DEFENSE:

What questions were you asked

84

8TH WITNESS:

    They asked me for more names

JUDGE:

    Were you beaten during the questioning

8TH WITNESS:

    Boger and Dylewski took turns
    with the bullwhip

COUNSEL FOR THE DEFENSE:

    Wasn't it the prisoners
    who did the beating

8TH WITNESS:

    I saw Boger and Dylewski
    with the whips in their hands

JUDGE:

    Where did they beat you

8TH WITNESS:

    On the buttocks
    back legs
    hands feet
    and the back of the head
    But they concentrated on
    the sexual organs
    They especially aimed for them
    I lost consciousness three times
    and they poured water on me

JUDGE:

    Accused Boger
    do you admit
    to having mistreated this witness

ACCUSED #2:

    There is only one answer to that
    a loud and definite no

8TH WITNESS:

    I still have the scars from it

ACCUSED #2:

    But not from me

JUDGE:

In the course of your interrogation
did you ever make use
of the instrument here described

ACCUSED #2:

There were times
when I had to arrange for its use
The punishment
was carried out by special-duty prisoners
under my supervision

JUDGE:

Do you regard
the witness' description
as untruthful

ACCUSED #2:

The description leaves out a great deal
and in many respects fails
to conform to the truth

JUDGE:

What was the truth

ACCUSED #2:

The moment the prisoner confessed
punishment was discontinued

JUDGE:

And if the prisoner did not confess

ACCUSED #2:

He was beaten until he bled
That was it

JUDGE:

Was a doctor present

ACCUSED #2:

I never saw an order
requiring the presence of a doctor
nor was it necessary
because the instant blood began to flow
I stopped

The purpose of the intensive interrogation
was achieved
when blood ran down their pants

JUDGE:

You felt you were fully justified
in carrying out these
intensive interrogations

ACCUSED #2:

They were clearly in line
with the duties and responsibilities
of my command
What's more it is my opinion
that even now corporal punishment
if administered
by juvenile courts for instance
would soon put a stop to a good deal
of delinquent behavior

COUNSEL FOR THE DEFENSE:

It has been stated by the witness
that no one could survive
the swing
From all appearances
this claim would seem to be exaggerated

8TH WITNESS:

When they took me down from the swing
Boger said
Now we've got you in shape
for a very pleasant heavenly ascension
I was taken to a cell in Barrack 11
I expected to be shot
at any time
I don't know
how many days I spent in there
The sores on my buttocks were festering
my testicles were blue and green
and tremendously swollen

Most of the time I was unconscious
Then I was taken to the washroom
with a number of other prisoners
We were told to strip
and our numbers were written
on our chests
with indelible ink
I knew that this
meant the death sentence
While we were standing there naked
the chief clerk came in and asked
how many prisoners should be crossed out
as executed
When he had left we were
recounted
There was one too many
I had learned always to be the last in line
Somebody kicked me
and I got my clothes back
I was to be taken back to the cell
to wait until the bunker was emptied again
but a prisoner orderly
took me with him to the infirmary
Sometimes
one of us did survive
and I
am one of those few who did

THE SONG OF
THE POSSIBILITY OF SURVIVAL

I

3RD WITNESS:
    The mood of the camp changed
    from one day to the next
    It depended on the mood
    of the commanding officer
    the adjutant
    and the Barrack-leader
    and it depended
    on how the war was going at the time
    At the beginning
    when they were still winning
    we were shoved around treated with contempt
    but they could still joke when they hit us
    But as the number of retreats
    and defeats mounted
    camp operations were stepped up
    Still you never knew
    what was going to happen
    An order to fall out could mean anything
    standing there for nothing
    or getting harassed
    In the infirmary
    prisoners could get treatment until
    they were well again and even
    be put on a special diet
    only to be sent up through the chimney

as soon as they had recovered
One of the prisoner orderlies was
beaten up by the camp doctor
because he had left out some minor detail
from a patient's chart
Meanwhile
the patient had already been killed
It was only by accident
that I
escaped the gassing
The ovens happened to be stopped up
that night
On the way back from the crematorium
the doctor who accompanied us found out
I was a medical student
and he found a place for me in his ward

JUDGE:

What was this doctor's name

3RD WITNESS:

Dr Vetter
He was a very well-bred man
Dr Schatz and Dr Frank
were also friendly to the prisoners
they delivered up to be killed
They did not kill out of hatred
or conviction
They killed only because they had to
and there was no point in discussing that
Only a few killed with passion
Boger was one of them
I saw prisoners
when they were called into Boger's room
and I saw them
when they came out
And when they were taken out to be shot
I heard Boger say with pride

These are mine
One prisoner who had been shot
was taken to the hospital
with an order from Boger
That man's life must be saved
so he can be hung
But the prisoner died in the hospital

JUDGE:

Does the accused Boger
recall this case

ACCUSED #2:

It was standard procedure that
prisoners wounded while attempting escape
were taken to the hospital
so they could be interrogated
when they had recovered
To that extent the witness' statement can
be considered absolutely correct
In this case I passed on the order
that the prisoner should be kept alive
I said
He must be saved
so he can be interrogated

JUDGE:

Was he to be hanged after that

ACCUSED #2:

That's possible
but that was not within my jurisdiction

6TH WITNESS:

Boger and Kaduk
carried out hangings on their own
Once 12 prisoners were
to be executed
as a reprisal for the escape of a prisoner
Boger and Kaduk

put the noose
over the prisoners' heads
COUNSEL FOR THE DEFENSE:
How do you know that
6TH WITNESS:
We stood on the assembly ground
We were ordered to watch
The prisoners shouted something
Boger and Kaduk went wild with rage
They started to kick
and slap them
then they hung on the prisoners' legs
and pulled them down
ACCUSED #2:
All I recall of this incident
is that one of the sentenced
broke away
while he was being taken out
under strict guard
to be executed
He lunged at me
so hard he broke one of my ribs
He was overpowered
He was bound
and I read the sentence
JUDGE:
Did the witness
hear the reading of a sentence
6TH WITNESS:
No sentence was read
ACCUSED #2:
Of course it was hard to hear the sentence
because the prisoners were shouting
PROSECUTING ATTORNEY:
What were they shouting

ACCUSED #2:
  Political slogans
PROSECUTING ATTORNEY:
  Of what kind
ACCUSED #2:
  They were inciting the prisoners against us
COUNSEL FOR THE DEFENSE:
  How did the prisoners react
ACCUSED #2:
  There were no observable incidents
  The sentence was executed
  as were all sentences
  I did not carry out
  the execution myself
  That was done by special-duty Kapos
COUNSEL FOR THE DEFENSE:
  Isn't it possible
  that the witness simply failed to hear
  the reading of the sentence
6TH WITNESS:
  The execution took place
  immediately after the escape
  There was no time
  for the case to be considered
  by a central office
  and for a sentence to be handed down
JUDGE:
  Was the commanding officer
  or his adjutant present
6TH WITNESS:
  Ranking officers were always present
  at public executions
  They wore white gloves
  on such occasions
  I can't say definitely
  whether the adjutant was present

Still it can be taken for granted
since he was responsible
for the execution of all orders
within this area of command

JUDGE:

Does the witness
recognize the adjutant
among the accused

6TH WITNESS:

That one is Mulka

JUDGE:

Accused Mulka
were you
present at this or any other hanging

ACCUSED #1:

I had nothing to do
with any killing
of any kind

JUDGE:

Did you hear of the orders in question
or did you ever pass such orders on

ACCUSED #1:

I did hear of such orders
but I personally never passed them on

JUDGE:

When faced with such orders
what did you do

ACCUSED #1:

I was careful
not to trouble my superiors
with questions about the legality
of prisoner executions
that were brought to my attention
Ultimately of course
I had a responsibility

to my family
and to myself

PROSECUTING ATTORNEY:
Accused Mulka
did you ever see the gallows

ACCUSED #1:
I beg your pardon

PROSECUTING ATTORNEY:
I asked whether you ever saw the gallows

ACCUSED #1:
No
I never set foot in the camp

PROSECUTING ATTORNEY:
You mean to say
that you
as adjutant to the commanding officer
were never in the camp

ACCUSED #1:
That's the absolute truth
The nature of my work was exclusively
administrative
I stayed strictly
within the administrative-office area

PROSECUTING ATTORNEY:
Where was this

ACCUSED #1:
In the army barracks
outside of the camp proper

PROSECUTING ATTORNEY:
Couldn't you see
into the camp from there

ACCUSED #1:
I don't believe you could

PROSECUTING ATTORNEY:
Could the witness

give us an idea of how the outer buildings
were situated in relation to the camp
6TH WITNESS:
All the back windows
in the administrative buildings
looked out onto the camp
Directly behind the administration buildings
were the concrete posts
with the electrically charged barbed wire
10 yards from the posts was the first barrack
Right behind that one
the other barracks in three rows
The three rows 10 yards apart at the most
The view up the long streets
was unobstructed
PROSECUTING ATTORNEY:
Where were the gallows
6TH WITNESS:
On the assembly ground
in front of the camp kitchen
Just to the right
as you come in through the main gate
onto the main street
PROSECUTING ATTORNEY:
Would you describe the gallows
6TH WITNESS:
Three poles
with an iron rail across the top
PROSECUTING ATTORNEY:
Accused Mulka
you lived in close proximity to the camp
According to camp regulations
your position entailed
reporting to the commanding officer
all important events within the camp
and processing all coded material

as well as instructing all guard units
as to the larger significance
of their assignment
Holding such a position
were you not aware of the punishments
carried out in the camp

ACCUSED #1:

Only once did I see
some sort of signed and dated order
authorizing corporal punishment

PROSECUTING ATTORNEY:

You were never required
to investigate
the reasons for the hangings and shootings

ACCUSED #1:

It wasn't my job
to concern myself with them

PROSECUTING ATTORNEY:

As adjutant to the camp commander
what were your duties then

ACCUSED #1:

I calculated operating costs
charted the distribution of the labor supply
and processed personnel files
I was also required to accompany
the commanding officer to receptions
and command the honor guard

PROSECUTING ATTORNEY:

When was the honor guard used

ACCUSED #1:

On ceremonial occasions
and for burials
A funeral procession
was trooped for the burials

PROSECUTING ATTORNEY:

Whose burial

ACCUSED #1:
    The burial of an officer
PROSECUTING ATTORNEY:
    Who was notified
    of deaths among the prisoners
ACCUSED #1:
    I don't know
    Perhaps the Political Division
PROSECUTING ATTORNEY:
    Weren't you informed
    that from 100 to 200 prisoners
    died daily in the camp
ACCUSED #1:
    I don't recall
    ever having seen
    comparative daily reports
    of the camp population
    On any given day
    10 or 15 discharges might be reported
    but numbers in the amount
    mentioned here
    I never heard
PROSECUTING ATTORNEY:
    You didn't know about the mass killings
    in the gas chambers
ACCUSED #1:
    I didn't know anything about them
PROSECUTING ATTORNEY:
    You never noticed the smoke
    from the chimneys of the crematoriums
    smoke that was visible for miles
ACCUSED #1:
    After all it was a big camp
    with its natural rate of discharge
    and they had to be burned

PROSECUTING ATTORNEY:
    You never noticed
    the condition of the prisoners
ACCUSED #1:
    It was a penal camp
    People weren't there for their health
PROSECUTING ATTORNEY:
    As adjutant to the camp's commanding officer
    weren't you interested in
    how the prisoners were fed and quartered
ACCUSED #1:
    I never heard of any complaints
PROSECUTING ATTORNEY:
    Didn't you ever discuss
    occurrences in the camp
    with your commanding officer
ACCUSED #1:
    No
    There were no exceptional occurrences
PROSECUTING ATTORNEY:
    From your point of view
    what was the purpose of the camp
ACCUSED #1:
    The purpose of a protective-custody camp
    was to educate enemies of the state
    to a different way of thinking
    It was not my job
    to question this purpose
PROSECUTING ATTORNEY:
    Did you know
    the significance of the designation
    special treatment
ACCUSED #1:
    That was a government secret
    of the highest priority
    I couldn't know anything about it

Anyone who spoke of it
risked the death penalty

PROSECUTING ATTORNEY:

Nevertheless you did know about it

ACCUSED #1:

I cannot answer that

PROSECUTING ATTORNEY:

What did you do for the troops

ACCUSED #1:

There was a theater and a movie house
and entertainment evenings
Mr Knittel took care of that
and also held evening classes
for the officers

PROSECUTING ATTORNEY:

Was he trained to do that

ACCUSED #1:

He was a high-school teacher
and if I am correctly informed
he is presently a principal
at a school somewhere
a man obviously suited
for the teaching profession

PROSECUTING ATTORNEY:

And you instructed
the troops in ideological matters

COUNSEL FOR THE DEFENSE:

We advise our client
that he need not reply
to questions put to him
by the assistant prosecuting attorney

PROSECUTING ATTORNEY:

The decision on this matter
rests solely
with the accused
By intervening at this point

the defense grossly exceeds
its legitimate authority
It is obvious
that by resorting to such tactics
the defense is attempting to prevent us
from determining the truth
COUNSEL FOR THE DEFENSE:
In reply to this astonishing performance
we must vigorously protest
At this point it becomes quite clear
that the prosecution
is not familiar with the rules obtaining in
these present proceedings
that they simply don't know the law
The prosecution
initiated these proceedings
already prejudiced
    [*The Accused laugh nodding in agree-
ment*]

THE SONG OF
THE POSSIBILITY OF SURVIVAL

II

3RD WITNESS:
    The power
    of any member of the camp personnel
    was unlimited
    They were free
    each one of them
    to kill
    or to save
    I saw Dr Flage standing by a fence
    with tears in his eyes
    looking at a trainload of children
    being taken to the crematorium
    He did nothing to stop me
    from holding on to the files
    of patients already selected
    and thus preventing their death
    Camp Doctor Flage showed me
    it was possible
    to see the one living person
    among the thousands
    He showed me
    that it would have been possible
    to influence the course of the camp operation
    if there had been others
    like him

COUNSEL FOR THE DEFENSE:
>   As a prisoner doctor
>   did you have the power to determine
>   whether your patient
>   should live or die

3RD WITNESS:
>   I could occasionally
>   save a life

COUNSEL FOR THE DEFENSE:
>   Yet weren't you also required
>   to select patients to be killed

3RD WITNESS:
>   There was nothing I could do
>   about changing the required quota
>   That was set by the camp administration
>   Still it was possible
>   to alter the lists

COUNSEL FOR THE DEFENSE:
>   When it came to choosing
>   between one patient and another
>   what determined your choice

3RD WITNESS:
>   We had to weigh
>   which of the two was more likely
>   to survive his illness
>   Then there was the far
>   more difficult question
>   which of the two would be useful
>   to the internal affairs of the prisoners

COUNSEL FOR THE DEFENSE:
>   Were some especially preferred

3RD WITNESS:
>   Politically active prisoners
>   naturally stuck together
>   supported and helped each other

as much as they could
Since I belonged to the resistance movement
within the camp
I of course did all I could
to keep others in the movement alive

COUNSEL FOR THE DEFENSE:

What could the resistance movement
accomplish in the camp

3RD WITNESS:

The chief aim of the resistance
was to keep alive our sense of solidarity
Furthermore we documented
everything that went on in the camp
and buried our evidence
in tin cans

COUNSEL FOR THE DEFENSE:

Did you have any contact with partisans
or any connection with the outside world

3RD WITNESS:

Prisoners assigned to factory work
could occasionally establish contact
with partisans
and they were able to give us reports
about the situation at the various fronts

COUNSEL FOR THE DEFENSE:

Were preparations made
for an armed rising in the camp

3RD WITNESS:

We managed to
smuggle in dynamite later on

COUNSEL FOR THE DEFENSE:

Was the camp ever attacked
from the outside or by any groups inside

3RD WITNESS:

In the last winter of the war

104

the special commandos
that worked in the crematoriums
revolted
The revolt was unsuccessful
That was the only active attempt
From the outside
no attempt was made

COUNSEL FOR THE DEFENSE:

Did you ever request aid
through your contacts

3RD WITNESS:

Reports on conditions in the camp
were smuggled out time and again

COUNSEL FOR THE DEFENSE:

What did you hope would come
of getting these reports out

3RD WITNESS:

We hoped for an air raid
on the gas chambers
or that the railroad tracks
leading
into the camp
would be bombed

COUNSEL FOR THE DEFENSE:

When you saw
that you were left quite alone
every form of military assistance denied you
how were you able to sustain
your will to resist

3RD WITNESS:

Considering our situation
it was resistance enough
just to keep alert
and never give up the thought
that someday there would come a time

when we could speak out
and tell what we had seen
and lived through

COUNSEL FOR THE DEFENSE:
How did you
justify what you had to do
with the oath you had taken as a doctor

PROSECUTING ATTORNEY:
We object to this question
which the defense has raised
solely to blur the distinction between
witness and accused
The accused killed of their own free choice
The witness was forced
to be present at the killings

3RD WITNESS:
I would like to reply to the question
Those prisoners who
by their privileged position in the camp
managed to postpone their own death
had at least to some degree
defied their masters
In order to maintain the possibility of survival
they were forced
to give the appearance of cooperating
I saw that demonstrated very clearly
in the infirmary
I soon became bound to the staff doctors
not only because of our professional relationship
but also through my complicity
in the workings of the camp system
Every prisoner
from those who held the most privileged posi-
tions

down to those who were dying
was part of that system
The difference
between us and the camp personnel
was less than what separated us
from those who were outside

COUNSEL FOR THE DEFENSE:

Do you mean to say
there was an understanding
between the administration and the prisoner

3RD WITNESS:

When we talk of our experience nowadays
with people who never were in a camp
there is always something
inconceivable to them about it
And yet they are the same people
who in the camp were prisoners and guards
Since such a great number of us
came into the camp
and since the number of those
who brought us there was also great
one would think that what happened then
would still be comprehensible today
Many of those who were destined
to play the part of prisoners
had grown up with the same ideas
the same way of looking at things
as those
who found themselves acting as guards
They were all equally dedicated
to the same nation
to its prosperity
and its rewards
And if they had not been designated
prisoners

they could equally well have been guards
We must drop the lofty view
that the camp world
is incomprehensible to us
We all knew the society
that produced a government
capable of creating such camps
The order that prevailed there
was an order whose basic nature
we were familiar with
For that very reason
we were able to find our way about
in its logical and ultimate consequence
where the oppressor
could expand his authority
to a degree never known before
and the oppressed
was forced to yield up
the fertilizing dust
of his bones

COUNSEL FOR THE DEFENSE:
We utterly reject
theories of this kind
theories that reflect
a completely distorted
ideological point of view

3RD WITNESS:
It is true
most of the prisoners
spilling out of the freight cars
onto the platform
had no time to comprehend
what was happening to them
Baffled and speechless
they walked that final path

and let themselves be killed
because they understood nothing
We call them heroes
but their death was pointless
We can see them before us
these millions
lit by searchlights
standing in a din of curses
and barking dogs
Today the outside world wonders
how they could have
let themselves be destroyed that way
We
who still live with these pictures
know that millions could stand again
waiting to be destroyed
and that the new destruction
will be far more efficient
than the old one was

COUNSEL FOR THE DEFENSE:
Was the witness
politically active
even before being sent
to the camp

3RD WITNESS:
Yes
It was our strength
that we knew
why we were there
It helped us
preserve our identity
But even that strength
sustained only a handful
to the moment of their death
They could be broken too

7TH WITNESS:
>There were 1200 of us
>who were led off to the crematoriums
>We had to wait a long time
>since there was another shipment
>ahead of us
>I was standing a little to one side
>A prisoner walked by
>He was very young
>He whispered
>Get away from here
>I picked up my shoes and walked off
>I went around a corner
>There was another prisoner there
>Where are you going
>he asked
>They sent me away
>I answered
>Then come with me
>he said
>So I got back into the camp

COUNSEL FOR THE DEFENSE:
>Was it that simple
>You could just walk away

7TH WITNESS:
>I don't know how it was with others
>I walked off
>and went into the infirmary
>The prisoner doctor asked me
>Do you want to live
>I said yes
>He looked at me for a while
>then he found a place for me there

COUNSEL FOR THE DEFENSE:
>And so you survived
>your stay in the camp

7TH WITNESS:

I came out of the camp
yes
but the camp is still there

THE SONG OF
THE POSSIBILITY OF SURVIVAL

III

JUDGE:
> The witness
> spent several months
> in women's Barrack Number 10
> Medical experiments
> were made there
> What can you tell us about them

4TH WITNESS:
> [*Remains silent*]

JUDGE:
> The court can well understand
> that you must find it difficult to speak
> and that you prefer to remain silent
> Yet we request you
> to search your memory
> for anything that may
> shed light on the events
> under consideration here today

4TH WITNESS:
> There were about 600 of us there
> Professor Clauberg directed the research
> The rest of the camp doctors supplied him
> with the subjects he worked on

JUDGE:
> Could you describe the experiments

4TH WITNESS:

 [*Remains silent*]

COUNSEL FOR THE DEFENSE:

 Does the witness
 suffer from lapses of memory

4TH WITNESS:

 I have been ill
 since my time in the camp

COUNSEL FOR THE DEFENSE:

 What are the symptoms of your illness

4TH WITNESS:

 Dizzy spells and nausea
 Earlier I had to throw up in the bathroom
 because it smelled of chlorine
 Chlorine was poured over the corpses
 I can't stand to be in locked rooms

COUNSEL FOR THE DEFENSE:

 No loss of memory

4TH WITNESS:

 I would like to forget
 but I keep seeing it
 I would like to have the number on my arm
 removed
 In the summer
 when I wear sleeveless dresses
 people stare at it
 and I always see the same look
 in their eyes

COUNSEL FOR THE DEFENSE:

 What look

4TH WITNESS:

 Scorn

JUDGE:

 Does the witness
 feel she is still being persecuted

4TH WITNESS:
    [*Remains silent*]
JUDGE:
    What experiments
    does the witness recall
4TH WITNESS:
    There were girls there
    17 or 18 years old
    They were chosen
    from the healthiest prisoners
    They were used for X-ray experiments
JUDGE:
    Could you describe these experiments
4TH WITNESS:
    The girls were placed
    in front of the X-ray machines
    A metal plate was attached
    to their stomachs and buttocks
    The X-rays were directed at their ovaries
    which were burned out
    Burns and running sores developed
    on their stomachs and buttocks as a result
JUDGE:
    What was done with these girls
4TH WITNESS:
    Within the next three months
    they were operated on
    a number of times
JUDGE:
    What kind of operations were these
4TH WITNESS:
    Their ovaries and gonads
    were removed
JUDGE:
    Did the patients die

4TH WITNESS:

    If they didn't die during the experiment
    they died soon after
    After a few weeks the girls
    had changed completely
    They looked like old women

JUDGE:

    Could you
    tell us if any of the accused present
    took part in these experiments

4TH WITNESS:

    All the doctors came together daily
    in their quarters
    It would seem likely that at the least
    they knew what was going on

COUNSEL FOR THE DEFENSE:

    We strenuously object
    to loose allegations of this kind
    The mere fact that our clients
    were in the vicinity when these events oc-
      curred
    by no means
    implicates them as accessories

JUDGE:

    Would the witness
    tell us what other experiments were under-
      taken

4TH WITNESS:

    [*Remains silent*]

COUNSEL FOR THE DEFENSE:

    It is our opinion
    that because of the witness' obvious ill-health
    she is incapable
    of providing the court with credible evidence

PROSECUTING ATTORNEY:

    Could you

describe for the court other experiments
which you witnessed yourself

4TH WITNESS:

A syringe
with a tube attachment
was used to inject a fluid
into the womb

JUDGE:

What kind of fluid was it

4TH WITNESS:

It was a cement paste
that burned and hurt like labor pains
The women could only walk stooped
to the X-ray table
where a picture was taken

JUDGE:

What was the purpose of the injection

4TH WITNESS:

The fallopian tubes would be glued together
to prevent conception

JUDGE:

Were the same patients
subjected to repeated experiments

4TH WITNESS:

After the injection of the paste
a contract fluid
was injected for X-ray observation
Then the paste
was pumped in once again
This process
might be repeated many times
at three- to four-week intervals
Infection of the womb
or of the stomach lining
caused most of the deaths
I never saw anyone sterilize

medical instruments
between treatments
JUDGE:
How many such experiments would you estimate
were carried out
4TH WITNESS:
During the six months
I spent in Barrack Number 10
400
In connection with these experiments
there were others
in artificial insemination
If a woman got pregnant
an abortion was induced
JUDGE:
In what month of the pregnancy was that
done
4TH WITNESS:
In the seventh month
A variety of X-ray experiments were made
throughout the pregnancy
After the abortion
if by any chance the child was still alive
it was killed and dissected
COUNSEL FOR THE DEFENSE:
Are the witness' statements
based on hearsay
or on firsthand knowledge
4TH WITNESS:
I speak from personal experience
COUNSEL FOR THE DEFENSE:
What saved you then
4TH WITNESS:
The evacuation of the camp

THE SONG OF
THE DEATH OF LILI TOFLER

I

JUDGE:
    Is the name of Lili Tofler
    familiar to the witness
5TH WITNESS:
    Yes
    It is
    Lili Tofler was an unusually
    pretty girl
    She was arrested
    because she wrote a letter
    to a prisoner
    When she tried
    to smuggle it in to the prisoner
    the letter was found
    Lili Tofler was interrogated
    They wanted the prisoner's name
    Boger was in charge of the interrogation
    At his order
    Lili Tofler was taken to the prison bunker
    There she was stood up naked
    against the wall
    They went through the whole procedure
    time and again
    exactly as if she was going to be shot
    All the orders were called out
    but they didn't shoot

Finally she got down on her knees
and begged them to shoot her

JUDGE:

Was she shot

5TH WITNESS:

Yes

6TH WITNESS:

I was under bunker arrest
when Lili Tofler was brought in
with two other prisoners
who had been involved
in the smuggling of the letter
Once during that time
Jakob
the special-duty prisoner
in charge of the bunker
let me use the washroom
I saw the girl lying dead on the floor
Boger killed the other prisoners later
out in the courtyard

JUDGE:

Accused Boger
are you familiar with this case

ACCUSED #2:

That Lili Tofler was executed
is true
As a typist in the Political Division
she had access to confidential files
and was forbidden all contact
with other prisoners
I had nothing to do
with her being killed
I was as shaken to hear of her death
as the Bunker-Jakob
whose face was covered with tears

JUDGE:
>   Can you tell us
>   what was in the letter

ACCUSED #2:
>   No

JUDGE:
>   Does the witness
>   know what was in the letter

5TH WITNESS:
>   In the letter Lili Tofler asked
>   if they would ever be able
>   to go on living
>   after the things they had seen
>   and experienced there
>   I remember too
>   that she went on to ask her friend
>   if he had gotten her previous letter
>   She also wrote about some encouraging news
>   she had heard

COUNSEL FOR THE DEFENSE:
>   How did you come to know this

5TH WITNESS:
>   Lili Tofler was a friend of mine
>   We lived in the same barrack
>   She talked to me about the letter
>   Later I saw the letter
>   I worked in the Camp Registry Office
>   Lili Tofler's death certificate
>   was sent there
>   The letter was attached

JUDGE:
>   Did you know the prisoner
>   to whom the letter was addressed

5TH WITNESS:
>   Yes

JUDGE:
> Did Lili Tofler betray his name

5TH WITNESS:
No
The prisoners had to line up
on the assembly ground
Lili was supposed to pick him out
I remember exactly
even now
how she stood in front of him
looked into his eyes
and then went on
without saying a word

COUNSEL FOR THE DEFENSE:
Were you required to appear
for the line-up too

5TH WITNESS:
Yes

COUNSEL FOR THE DEFENSE:
Where was the assembly ground

5TH WITNESS:
It was the street and the open space
in front of the kitchen barracks
in the old camp

COUNSEL FOR THE DEFENSE:
Would you describe the assembly ground

5TH WITNESS:
To the right of the gallows
was the small guardhouse
where officers stood
to take the roll call
Its walls were wood
painted to look like stone
On top of the pitched roof
was a weathervane
It looked like a toy house

There were poplars on both sides of the street
The prisoners stood in the street
and in between the barracks
Lili Tofler was led along in front of them
It was on that same day
that I saw
what was painted on the kitchen roof
It was painted in large letters
THERE IS ONE WAY TO FREEDOM
ITS MILESTONES ARE
OBEDIENCE DILIGENCE CLEANLINESS
HONESTY TRUTHFULNESS
AND LOVE OF COUNTRY

JUDGE:
Was the prisoner
to whom the letter was addressed
ever discovered

5TH WITNESS:
No

THE SONG OF
THE DEATH OF LILI TOFLER

II

JUDGE:
  You were in charge
  of the agricultural operations of the camp
  At the time of her arrest
  Lili Tofler was working
  in one of the offices
  under your supervision
  What did she do there
1ST WITNESS:
  She did drafting
  or typing
  I can't remember which
JUDGE:
  Had she been transferred to you
  from the Political Division
1ST WITNESS:
  It's been so long now I couldn't say
  Our operation had no direct connection
  with the camp
  We were under the jurisdiction
  of the S.S. Office of Economy
  Since we were growing rubber plants
  our operations were essential
  to the war effort
  Basically my duties
  were of a purely scientific nature

JUDGE:
　　Do you recall
　　the arrest
　　of Lili Tofler
1ST WITNESS:
　　As I remember
　　it had something to do with a letter
JUDGE:
　　Do you know
　　that Lili Tofler was arrested
　　because of this letter
1ST WITNESS:
　　I believe
　　the letter was found in a shipment of carrots
JUDGE:
　　What was the shipment for
1ST WITNESS:
　　They were carrots we grew
　　for the medical section
JUDGE:
　　For what purpose
1ST WITNESS:
　　I assume
　　they were used for special diets
　　Professor Clauberg had ordered them
JUDGE:
　　What did you know
　　about Professor Clauberg's work
1ST WITNESS:
　　They carried out research there
　　commissioned by various
　　pharmaceutical concerns
JUDGE:
　　What kind of research
1ST WITNESS:
　　That I don't know

All I knew about the camp
was that it had to do with
a large industrial complex
and that its various branches
employed prisoners as labor supply

PROSECUTING ATTORNEY:

To which of these branches
did your operation belong

1ST WITNESS:

We were a subdivision of the Buna Works
of I-G Farben
We were engaged in war production

PROSECUTING ATTORNEY:

Were you aware
that prisoners had been projected
as the labor supply
when these industries were established

1ST WITNESS:

Yes
naturally

PROSECUTING ATTORNEY:

Did the industries
pay wages for prisoner labor

1ST WITNESS:

Of course they did
There were established rates

PROSECUTING ATTORNEY:

What were the rates

1ST WITNESS:

For a skilled worker a dollar a day
For an unskilled 75 cents

PROSECUTING ATTORNEY:

How long was the work day

1ST WITNESS:

11 hours

PROSECUTING ATTORNEY:

    To whom were the wages paid

1ST WITNESS:

    To the camp administration
    After all
    they had to provide for the prisoners

PROSECUTING ATTORNEY:

    Didn't you know
    that the prisoners were
    used up and then killed

1ST WITNESS:

    I always tried to help the prisoners
    more so in fact than I had any right to
    I suffered
    when I saw
    how the prisoners assigned to my operation
    had to walk all those miles every day
    from their barracks over to the work camp
    I made use
    of every available emergency measure
    to ensure that our prisoners
    got better care
    and a good pair of shoes

PROSECUTING ATTORNEY:

    How many prisoners were employed
    in your operation

1ST WITNESS:

    5 to 6 hundred

PROSECUTING ATTORNEY:

    Didn't you ever notice
    the frequent turnover
    in the make-up of the work details

1ST WITNESS:

    I did what I could
    to hold on to my people

PROSECUTING ATTORNEY:
    Did any of them get sick
1ST WITNESS:
    Naturally
    I knew of course about the epidemics
    that afflicted the prisoners in the camp
PROSECUTING ATTORNEY:
    You didn't notice
    that prisoners on the sick list
    never returned
1ST WITNESS:
    No
    Frequently they did come back
    from the infirmary
PROSECUTING ATTORNEY:
    Did you hear of any mistreatment in the
        camp
1ST WITNESS:
    Heard about it
    yes
PROSECUTING ATTORNEY:
    What did you hear
1ST WITNESS:
    I heard
    they were beaten
PROSECUTING ATTORNEY:
    Who beat them
1ST WITNESS:
    I don't know
    I never saw it happen
    I just heard about it
PROSECUTING ATTORNEY:
    Did you know about
    the extermination program
1ST WITNESS:
    If you were there three years

naturally something leaked out
You knew what was going on
but later on
when I heard the numbers involved
I simply couldn't grasp it

PROSECUTING ATTORNEY:

You never saw any of the transports

1ST WITNESS:

A couple of times at the most

PROSECUTING ATTORNEY:

Do you know any of the accused present here

1ST WITNESS:

I know some of them
Mainly the group leaders
We used to meet
in their club
on a purely social basis

PROSECUTING ATTORNEY:

Today you hold a high
advisory position in the government
Did you meet these men again
after the war
when most of them
had returned to civilian life

1ST WITNESS:

I may have met one or another of them

PROSECUTING ATTORNEY:

On such occasions
did you ever talk about
the events of those days

1ST WITNESS:

Mr Prosecutor
we were all concerned with
one thing
winning the war

128

PROSECUTING ATTORNEY:

The court has summoned as witnesses
three former directors
of factories attached to the camp
One of these witnesses
had submitted to the court a sworn affidavit
stating that he is blind
and therefore cannot appear
The second suffers from a fractured spine
Only one former chairman of the board
has come
Would the witness
tell us if he is still connected
with the firms
which formerly employed prisoners

COUNSEL FOR THE DEFENSE:

We object to this question
which has no other motive
than to undermine public confidence
in our industrial concerns

2ND WITNESS:

I am no longer actively engaged
in business

PROSECUTING ATTORNEY:

Do you receive a pension
from these concerns

2ND WITNESS:

Yes

PROSECUTING ATTORNEY:

Does this pension amount to
75,000 dollars a year

COUNSEL FOR THE DEFENSE:

We object to the question

PROSECUTING ATTORNEY:

Now that you live in your castle
and are no longer engaged

with the business of your concern
which has only changed by changing its name
what do you do
2ND WITNESS:

I collect porcelain
paintings and engravings
as well as various objects of folk art
COUNSEL FOR THE DEFENSE:

Questions of this nature
are entirely irrelevant
to the stated purpose of these proceedings
PROSECUTING ATTORNEY:

As a representative of the camp industries
you were directly responsible
for assigning prisoners to the factories
What can you tell us about the agreement
arrived at between these industries
and the camp administration
relating to prisoners
no longer fit for work
2ND WITNESS:

I know nothing about that
PROSECUTING ATTORNEY:

The court has in its possession
weekly reports which deal with prisoners
    found
by the management of these industries
to be too weak to do their work
2ND WITNESS:

I don't know anything about that
PROSECUTING ATTORNEY:

Didn't you ever notice the physical condition
of the prisoners
2ND WITNESS:

I personally did everything
I could to prevent the utilization

of a labor force
composed of asocial
or politically unreliable elements

PROSECUTING ATTORNEY:

The court has in its record
a letter which mentions
the happy and prosperous friendship
existing between your firm
and the camp administration
Among other things
the letter goes on to say
At dinner
we made further use of the occasion
to draw up measures
advantageous to the Buna works
that relate to the merger
of the truly outstanding
operations of the camp
What were those measures

2ND WITNESS:

I simply had to do my duty
and to see to it
that government requisitions
were met

PROSECUTING ATTORNEY:

Will you not
speak out clearly
to corroborate
what a previous witness pointed out
the system of exploitation
that existed in the camp
By the limitless grinding down of people
you
as well as the other directors
of the large firms involved

made profits
that annually amounted to billions

COUNSEL FOR THE DEFENSE:
Objection

PROSECUTING ATTORNEY:
Let us once more bring to mind
that the successors to those same concerns
have ended up today in magnificent condition
and that they are now in the midst of
as they say
a new phase of expansion

COUNSEL FOR THE DEFENSE:
We call upon the court
to make a record
of this slander

THE SONG OF
THE DEATH OF LILI TOFLER

III

JUDGE:
>   What do you know of the arrest
>   of Lili Tofler
1ST WITNESS:
>   I don't know what happened
>   All I remember is
>   that she was taken away
>   I asked what was going on and heard
>   they were still investigating the matter
>   Later I heard
>   they had killed her
JUDGE:
>   Who killed her
1ST WITNESS:
>   I don't know
>   I wasn't there
JUDGE:
>   You were at that time a brigadier general
>   which meant you ranked
>   between a colonel and a major general
>   Was there no way you could have intervened
>   when one of your workers was taken away
1ST WITNESS:
>   I wasn't
>   sufficiently informed about the case

JUDGE:

    You made no inquiries
    about the cause of her arrest

1ST WITNESS:

    That was beyond my jurisdiction

JUDGE:

    Yet that constituted a gross interference
    in your personal sphere of activity
    A person whom you needed
    for work essential to the war effort
    was simply removed from your laboratory

1ST WITNESS:

    Lili Tofler was not an outstanding worker

JUDGE:

    But you greatly outranked
    any man in the Political Division
    Why did you tolerate this invasion
    of your own area of responsibility

1ST WITNESS:

    Mr Chairman
    there was an unwritten law then
    that applied to everybody
    It was
    Take care about doing favors for prisoners
    You could go just so far
    but no further

JUDGE:

    The court calls as witness
    the prisoner
    to whom Lili Tofler
    wrote the previously mentioned letter
    Would you tell us
    how you managed to survive

9TH WITNESS:

    A few days after she had been
    taken to the bunker

I was brought there too
I thought
Lili had betrayed me
but I was just one of many
that had been brought in as hostages
I heard there
that every morning and every afternoon
Lili had to stand in the washroom for an hour
The whole time she was in there Boger kept
a pistol pressed against her head
That went on for four days
Then I was taken out
with a group of 50 prisoners
to be shot
All that time I thought
Boger must know
the letter was meant for me
I saw the clerk put a cross
next to my name on the list
On paper I was already dead
The prisoners were taken out to the yard
and shot
Only two
for some reason
were left behind
I was one of them
I was still in the hallway
when suddenly the Bunker-Jakob came
and pulled me back out into the yard
I thought
Now I'm going to be shot
But he just showed me the pile
of dead comrades
On top lay the two prisoners
who had smuggled the letter into the camp
Over to one side was Lili

with two holes in her heart
I asked Jakob
who had shot her
He said
Boger

JUDGE:
Accused Boger
do you have anything to add

ACCUSED #2:
No
thank you

JUDGE:
Where did Lili Tofler originally come from

5TH WITNESS:
I don't know where she came from

JUDGE:
What was she like

5TH WITNESS:
Whenever I met Lili
and asked her
How are you Lili
she said
Fine
I am always fine

THE SONG OF
S.S. CORPORAL STARK

I

8TH WITNESS:
>   The accused Stark
>   was in charge of the Reception Squad
>   I was assigned to the squad as a clerk
>   Stark was 20 years old then
>   In his free time
>   he used to study for his high-school finals
>   To test himself on the subjects
>   Stark enjoyed putting all sorts of questions
>   to the college graduates among the prisoners
>   On the evening
>   the Polish woman with the two children
>   was brought in
>   he was discussing
>   aspects of humanism in Goethe with us

JUDGE:
>   What was the reason
>   for their being brought in

8TH WITNESS:
>   We only found that out later
>   The eight-year-old boy
>   had picked up a rabbit and given it
>   to the woman's two-year-old daughter
>   to play with
>   The rabbit belonged to a camp official
>   So all three

were to be shot
Stark
carried out the execution
JUDGE:
Could you see the execution
8TH WITNESS:
Executions were carried out
in the old crematorium in those days
The crematorium was directly
behind the reception barrack
Through the window
we could see Stark
with the woman and two children
go into the crematorium
He had his rifle slung over his shoulder
We heard a series of shots
Then Stark came out alone
JUDGE:
Accused Stark
does this description correspond to the facts
ACCUSED #12:
I completely reject it
JUDGE:
What was your rank in the camp
ACCUSED #12:
I was barrack-leader
JUDGE:
How did you come there
ACCUSED #12:
I was assigned to camp duty
along with a group
of other noncommissioned officers
JUDGE:
Were you made barrack-leader
right from the start

ACCUSED #12:

That's what we were meant for
that's what we were used for

JUDGE:

Were you trained
for this assignment

ACCUSED #12:

We had our leadership course behind us

JUDGE:

Were you given any general instructions
for your task in the camp

ACCUSED #12:

Only a short indoctrination period

JUDGE:

What happened when you arrived at the
camp

ACCUSED #12:

There was a reception commission

JUDGE:

Made up of whom

ACCUSED #12:

The commanding officer and the adjutant
the protective-custody camp leader
and the chief clerk

JUDGE:

What assignment were you given

ACCUSED #12:

I was first assigned to a prisoner barrack
Most of them were young
High-school and university students

JUDGE:

Why were they in the camp

ACCUSED #12:

I believe
it was because of their contact
with the resistance movement

It was a collective sentence
They had been transferred there
by Security Police Command Headquarters
JUDGE:
    Did you see their admission orders
ACCUSED #12:
    No
    It wasn't any of my business either
JUDGE:
    What did you have to do then
ACCUSED #12:
    I had to see to it
    that the people got to work on time
    and that the numbers checked out
JUDGE:
    Were there any attempts to escape
ACCUSED #12:
    Not under my command
JUDGE:
    Were the people adequately provided for
ACCUSED #12:
    They each got their quart of soup
JUDGE:
    What happened
    if the people could not
    or would not work
ACCUSED #12:
    That didn't happen
JUDGE:
    Didn't you ever have cause to take action
    when prisoners broke rules
ACCUSED #12:
    That never came up
    I never had to turn in a report
JUDGE:
    You never struck anyone

ACCUSED #12:
     I never had to
JUDGE:
     When were you transferred
     to the Reception Section
     of the Political Division
ACCUSED #12:
     May 1941
JUDGE:
     What was the reason
     for your being transferred
ACCUSED #12:
     I used to go riding
     One of the men I got to know that way
     was the chief of the Political Division
     Lieutenant Grabner
     He asked me what I was by profession
     When I told him I was a student
     studying for my final exams
     he said
     they were looking for people like me
     A few days later
     I received my transfer orders
JUDGE:
     What were your duties
     in the Reception Section
ACCUSED #12:
     The first thing I had to do
     was to familiarize myself
     with the registration
     Incoming prisoners were
     provided with a number
     After that
     personnel records had to be set up
     and index cards filled out

JUDGE:

How did the prisoners arrive

ACCUSED #12:

They were marched in
trucked in
or they came by train
Trains arrived every Tuesday
Thursday and Friday

JUDGE:

What was the reception procedure

ACCUSED #12:

I had to stand by
when transports were announced
First
prisoners were assembled
in front of the camp entrance
then the transport leader
handed over the transport papers
to Reception
Prisoners fell in for the count
and were issued their numbers
At that time
numbers were not yet tattooed
Each prisoner was issued a number
in triplicate on cardboard
One number he kept
one went with personal effects
one was attached to valuables
He had to retain his cardboard number
until he was issued a cloth one

JUDGE:

What was your part in this procedure

ACCUSED #12:

I handed out the numbers
and conducted the prisoners
to the personal-effects barrack

There prisoners were stripped
showered and dressed
Their hair was cut
Then they were received
by Reception

JUDGE:

What did that entail

ACCUSED #12:

Personnel records were filled out
Questionnaires made up for Reception
were taken to the Reception office
An admissions list was then drawn up
listing the different categories
political prisoners
criminal prisoners
and racial prisoners
This list was then circulated
to the various sections

JUDGE:

To which sections

ACCUSED #12:

To the protective-custody camp leader
to headquarters
to the Political Division
and to the doctors
12 copies went out for distribution
with the daily dispatches

JUDGE:

Did you have anything more to do
with the prisoners

ACCUSED #12:

After Reception
for me they were over and done with

PROSECUTING ATTORNEY:

Accused Stark

were you on hand
for the arrival of all transports

ACCUSED #12:
It was my duty to be present

PROSECUTING ATTORNEY:
When transports arrived
what were your duties

ACCUSED #12:
All I had to do there
was manage the record traffic

PROSECUTING ATTORNEY:
What does that mean

ACCUSED #12:
Some of the prisoners were held over
These I had to enter in the book

PROSECUTING ATTORNEY:
And the others

ACCUSED #12:
The others were transferred

PROSECUTING ATTORNEY:
What was the difference

ACCUSED #12:
Prisoners held over
went to the camp
Transferred prisoners
were neither received
nor admitted
That is the difference
between held over
and transferred

PROSECUTING ATTORNEY:
What happened to the transferred prisoners

ACCUSED #12:
They were taken directly
to the small crematorium
for extermination

PROSECUTING ATTORNEY:
    Was this before the construction
    of the big crematoriums
ACCUSED #12:
    The big crematoriums in the outer camp
    first went into operation
    in the summer of 1942
    Until then the crematorium
    in the old camp was used
PROSECUTING ATTORNEY:
    How were the prisoners transferred
ACCUSED #12:
    Lists were compared
    and names crossed out
    Prisoners who were not
    to be received into the camp
    were marched into the small crematorium
PROSECUTING ATTORNEY:
    What were they told
ACCUSED #12:
    They were informed
    that they were going to be disinfected
PROSECUTING ATTORNEY:
    Weren't they uneasy
ACCUSED #12:
    No
    They went in quietly

THE SONG OF
S.S. CORPORAL STARK

II

8TH WITNESS:
 We knew exactly how Stark would behave
 when he came back from a killing
 Everything in the room
 had to be in order and absolutely clean
 and we had to chase the flies out
 with handkerchiefs
 If he spotted a fly
 he would go into a rage
 Even before he took off his cap
 he would wash his hands in a basin
 his flunkey always had ready for him
 on a stool next to the door
 When he had washed his hands
 he pointed at the dirty water
 and the flunkey had to run out
 for more
 Then he handed us his jacket to be cleaned
 and washed his hands and face again

7TH WITNESS:
 I see Stark always
 all the time
 I can hear him call
 Move
 get in

move you pigs
And then we had to go into the chamber
JUDGE:
What chamber
7TH WITNESS:
The chamber in the old crematorium
Several hundred
women and children
lay there like packages
There were prisoners of war in there too
Move
Get their clothes off
Stark yelled
I was 18 years old
and I had never seen a corpse before
I just stood there
Then Stark started beating me
JUDGE:
Were there wounds on the dead
7TH WITNESS:
Yes
JUDGE:
Were they bullet wounds
7TH WITNESS:
No
They had been gassed
They were heaped up stiff
on top of each other
Sometimes when we pulled
their clothes ripped
Then we were beaten again
JUDGE:
Weren't the people required
to undress first
7TH WITNESS:
That was later

in the new crematoriums
where there were rooms for that
JUDGE:
Was Stark present there too
7TH WITNESS:
Stark was always present
I can hear him shouting
Move
Get those rags
Once a small man hid himself
under a pile of clothes
Stark found him
Come here he shouted
and pushed him up against the wall
He shot him first in one leg
and then in the other
Finally he slid down on a bench
and then Stark shot him dead
He always liked to shoot the legs first
Once I heard a woman scream
Captain
I didn't do anything
He yelled
Get up against the wall Sarah
The woman begged him not to kill her
Then he started shooting
JUDGE:
When did you
first see the accused Stark
at these killings
7TH WITNESS:
In the fall of 1941
JUDGE:
Were these the first killings
by gas

7TH WITNESS:
>> Yes
JUDGE:
>> Would you describe the old crematorium
7TH WITNESS:
>> It was built of concrete
>> It had a thick square chimney
>> The walls were covered by
>> sloping embankments
>> The chamber was about 20 yards long
>> and five yards wide
>> You had to pass through a small anteroom
>>> first
>> On the other side of the chamber
>> a door led to the first oven
>> and a second door to a room
>> with the two other ovens
JUDGE:
>> Accused Stark
>> how large were the groups
>> you had to conduct to the crematoriums
ACCUSED #12:
>> On the average
>> 150 to 200 head
JUDGE:
>> Were women and children among them
ACCUSED #12:
>> Yes
JUDGE:
>> Did you think it right
>> that women and children
>> should be a part of these transports
ACCUSED #12:
>> Yes
>> The Family Liability Laws
>> were in effect then

JUDGE:
> You did not question
> the guilt of these women and children

ACCUSED #12:
> We had been told
> they had actively participated
> in poisoning springs and wells
> blowing up bridges
> and other acts of sabotage

JUDGE:
> Did you also see prisoners of war
> among these people

ACCUSED #12:
> Yes
> Those prisoners had
> by issued order
> lost all claim to decent treatment

PROSECUTING ATTORNEY:
> Accused Stark
> in the fall of 1941
> a large number of Soviet
> prisoners of war
> were brought to the camp
> According to court records
> you were instrumental
> in processing these contingents

ACCUSED #12:
> In connection with these transports
> I only followed instructions

PROSECUTING ATTORNEY:
> What did that mean

ACCUSED #12:
> I simply had to march them off
> take over their cards marked
> for execution

destroy their identification tags
and enter their numbers in the file

PROSECUTING ATTORNEY:

What reason
was given for the execution
of these prisoners of war

ACCUSED #12:

We were dealing with the annihilation
of an ideology
With their fanatical political orientation
these prisoners constituted a threat
to camp security

PROSECUTING ATTORNEY:

Where were the executions carried out

ACCUSED #12:

In the courtyard of Barrack 11

PROSECUTING ATTORNEY:

Did you take part in the executions

ACCUSED #12:

In one instance
yes

PROSECUTING ATTORNEY:

What was the procedure

ACCUSED #12:

The roll was called
and the formalities concluded
They were taken out to the courtyard
one after the other
It was almost over
Then Grabner said
Stark you carry on
Up to then the other corporals
had been taking turns

PROSECUTING ATTORNEY:

How many did you shoot

ACCUSED #12:
    I can't remember
PROSECUTING ATTORNEY:
    More than one
ACCUSED #12:
    Yes
PROSECUTING ATTORNEY:
    More than two
ACCUSED #12:
    Four or five possibly
PROSECUTING ATTORNEY:
    Did you try
    to get out of taking part in the execution
ACCUSED #12:
    But it was an order
    It was my duty as a soldier
PROSECUTING ATTORNEY:
    Did you participate
    in any other executions
ACCUSED #12:
    No
    I was given leave
    to complete my studies
PROSECUTING ATTORNEY:
    When did your leave begin
ACCUSED #12:
    In December 1941
PROSECUTING ATTORNEY:
    When did you complete your studies
ACCUSED #12:
    I passed my examinations
    in the spring of 1942
PROSECUTING ATTORNEY:
    Did you then
    return to the camp

ACCUSED #12:
    For a short time yes
COUNSEL FOR THE DEFENSE:
    We would like to call
    to the attention of the court
    the fact that our client
    was 20 years old
    when he was ordered
    to camp duty
    As witnesses have substantiated
    our client had keen intellectual interests
    and his whole personality
    made him utterly unfit
    for the task assigned him
    We would like to call attention to the fact
    that one year after completing
    his secondary schooling
    our client
    was granted a further period of leave
    to study law
    In the last year of the war
    he was wounded in front-line action
    Immediately after the war
    as soon as he was able to settle down
    in more normal conditions
    he went on to develop in exemplary fashion
    He studied agriculture
    passed his assessor's examination
    was an expert
    with the Economic Advisory Council
    and until his arrest
    was an instructor
    in an agricultural school
PROSECUTING ATTORNEY:
    Accused Stark
    did you take part in the first gassings

which were carried out
on Soviet prisoners of war
in the first weeks of September 1941
ACCUSED #12:
No
PROSECUTING ATTORNEY:
Large-scale extermination
of Soviet prisoners of war began
in the fall and winter of 1941
These resulted in the death of 25,000 men
You processed these prisoners
You knew of their death
you consented to their death
and you performed
essential parts of the operation
COUNSEL FOR THE DEFENSE:
We strongly protest
these attacks on our client
Such wholesale accusations
are completely meaningless
Only clear-cut proofs of criminal acts
or conspiracy in committing such acts
in relation to the charges of murder
are relevant to these proceedings
Wherever there is the slightest doubt
the benefit must be given to the accused
[*The Accused laugh nodding in
agreement*]

THE SONG OF
S.S. CORPORAL STARK

III

JUDGE:
> Accused Stark
> you never once took part in the gassings

ACCUSED #12:
> There was one time I had to

JUDGE:
> How many prisoners were involved

ACCUSED #12:
> Somewhere around 150
> Four truckloads anyway

JUDGE:
> Who were the prisoners

ACCUSED #12:
> It was a mixed transport

JUDGE:
> What was your job

ACCUSED #12:
> I stood outside by the stairs
> after I had led them
> into the crematorium
> The medical orderlies
> in charge of the gassing
> had locked the doors
> and were making the necessary preparations

JUDGE:
> What kind of preparations

ACCUSED #12:

They got out the cans
and put on their gas masks
Then they went up the embankment
to the roof deck
Usually it took four men to do the job
This time there were only three
and they called back
they needed somebody to help them out
Since I was the only one around
Grabner said
Move
give them a hand
Then the camp leader came over
and said rather sharply
If you don't go up there
in you go
So I had to go up
and help pour

JUDGE:

Where was the gas thrown in

ACCUSED #12:

Through vents in the deck

JUDGE:

What did the people in the chamber below
do then

ACCUSED #12:

I don't know

JUDGE:

You didn't hear anything
of what was going on down there

ACCUSED #12:

They screamed

JUDGE:

For how long

ACCUSED #12:

 Around 10 or 15 minutes

JUDGE:

 Who opened the chamber afterward

ACCUSED #12:

 One of the orderlies

JUDGE:

 What did you see in there

ACCUSED #12:

 I didn't take a very close look

JUDGE:

 Did you see anything wrong
 with what you saw there

ACCUSED #12:

 No
 not at all
 Only the way it was done

JUDGE:

 What do you mean

ACCUSED #12:

 If they had been shot
 it would have been one thing
 But the use of gas
 was unmanly and cowardly

JUDGE:

 Accused Stark
 during the course of your duties
 didn't you ever have any doubts
 about your conduct in the camp

ACCUSED #12:

 Your Honor
 I would like to explain that
 Every third word we heard
 even back in grammar school
 was about
 how they

were to blame for everything
and how they
ought to be weeded out
It was hammered into us
that this would only be for the good
of our people
In leadership school
we were taught above all
to accept everything
without question
If anybody did raise a question
they were told
What is being done
is done strictly according to the law
It's no use saying
the laws are different now
We were told
You've got to study
You've got to have an education
It's more important than food
Your Honor
we weren't supposed to think for ourselves
There were others around
to do our thinking for us
[*Assenting laughter from the Accused*]

END OF PART I

THE SONG OF THE BLACK WALL

I

3RD WITNESS:
> Executions were
> carried out in front of the Black Wall
> in the yard of Barrack 11

JUDGE:
> Where was Barrack 11

3RD WITNESS:
> At the far right end
> of the old camp

JUDGE:
> Can the witness
> describe the yard

3RD WITNESS:
> It was between Barrack 10 and Barrack 11
> and took up a whole barrack length
> about 40 yards
> It was closed off at both ends
> by brick walls

JUDGE:
> How did one enter the yard

3RD WITNESS:
> Through a side door from Barrack 11
> or through the gate in the front brick wall

JUDGE:
> Was there any way of seeing into the yard

3RD WITNESS:
> Only through the ground-floor windows

at the front of Barrack 11
When the gate was opened
to remove the dead
there was a curfew
All the other windows in Barrack 11
were bricked up except for a crack at the top
Windows in the women's barrack
on the other side
were boarded up

JUDGE:
How high was the wall

3RD WITNESS:
About 14 feet high

JUDGE:
And where was the Black Wall

3RD WITNESS:
Opposite the front gate
against the back wall

JUDGE:
What did the Black Wall look like

3RD WITNESS:
It was made out of thick planks
covered with tarred canvas
Bullet-proof walls
came out at an angle from the back

JUDGE:
How large was the Black Wall

3RD WITNESS:
About 10 feet high
13 wide

JUDGE:
From where were sentenced prisoners
brought out to the Black Wall

3RD WITNESS:
They came out through the side door
of Barrack 11

JUDGE:

Describe the procedure

3RD WITNESS:

The Bunker-Jakob led out
two prisoners at a time
The prisoners were naked

JUDGE:

Who was this Bunker-Jakob

3RD WITNESS:

He was the special-duty prisoner
assigned to Barrack 11
He was a big powerfully built man
a former boxer

JUDGE:

How were the prisoners brought out

3RD WITNESS:

Jakob was in the middle
holding them by the arm

JUDGE:

Were the prisoners' hands bound

3RD WITNESS:

Up until 1942 they were
tied behind the back with wire
Later they stopped using it
since experience showed that most prisoners
went along quietly

JUDGE:

How far was it from the side door
to the Black Wall

3RD WITNESS:

First the six steps down from the door
then 20 paces to the Black Wall
Everything went at the double
When Jakob had brought
the prisoners to the wall

he ran back
to get the next two

JUDGE:

How were the executions carried out

3RD WITNESS:

Prisoners were put
face to the wall
three to six feet apart
The executioner went up to the first one
put his gun against the prisoner's neck
then fired from about four inches off
The other prisoner saw it
As soon as the first had fallen
it was his turn

JUDGE:

What kind of weapon
was used

3RD WITNESS:

A small-caliber rifle with a silencer

JUDGE:

Whom did you see
at the Black Wall executions

3RD WITNESS:

The camp commander
the adjutant
the head of the Political Division Grabner
and his assistants
Among others I saw Broad Stark
Boger and Schlage
Kaduk was frequently there too

COUNSEL FOR THE DEFENSE:

Are you sure
the adjutant was there

3RD WITNESS:

He was a familiar figure

We knew the camp commander
We knew his adjutant just as well

COUNSEL FOR THE DEFENSE:
During the executions
what were your duties in the yard

3RD WITNESS:
As a medical student
I was assigned to the corpse-bearers' detail

JUDGE:
Which of the accused
took part in the executions

3RD WITNESS:
Boger Broad Stark Schlage and Kaduk
I saw them carry out executions on their own

JUDGE:
Accused Boger
did you take part in executions
carried out at the Black Wall

ACCUSED #2:
I never fired a shot in the camp

JUDGE:
Accused Broad
did you take part in executions
carried out at the Black Wall

ACCUSED #16:
I was never required to carry out
such assignments

JUDGE:
Accused Schlage
as supervisor of Barrack 11
did you
take part in executions
carried out at the Black Wall

ACCUSED #14:
I was not authorized to do so

JUDGE:

> Accused Kaduk
> did you take part in executions
> carried out at the Black Wall

ACCUSED #7:

> I never set foot in Barrack 11
> What has been said here about me
> is nothing but a lie

JUDGE:

> Can the witness tell us
> if death sentences
> were read out before the executions

3RD WITNESS:

> Not usually
> When there was a death sentence
> a special execution squad appeared
> but I can only recall that happening
> in a few cases
> Generally prisoners were
> just hauled out of the cells in Barrack 11

JUDGE:

> What condition were the prisoners in

3RD WITNESS:

> Most of them were badly injured
> after the interrogations
> and after their time in the Bunker
> Some
> had to be carried out to the Wall
> on stretchers

JUDGE:

> We call as witness
> the then ranking officer
> of the accused here present
> As head of the Central Office
> of the Security Police attached to the camp

and presiding officer at its summary court
what did you have to do
with the executions carried out
by the Political Division

1ST WITNESS:

My post had no connection whatsoever
with the functioning
of the Political Division within the camp
I dealt exclusively with cases
relating to partisan resistance
These were brought over to the camp
and trial was held there in a hearing room

JUDGE:

Where was this room

1ST WITNESS:

In one of the barracks

JUDGE:

Was it not in Barrack 11

1ST WITNESS:

That's more than I can remember

6TH WITNESS:

I was the clerk in Barrack 11
My job gave me an idea
of the working of the summary courts
Court sessions were held in a room
on the front left side of Barrack 11

JUDGE:

What was the room like

6TH WITNESS:

There were four windows onto the courtyard
and a long table

JUDGE:

Do you recall this room

1ST WITNESS:

No

JUDGE:
    Did you ever go into the inner area
    of the old camp
1ST WITNESS:
    That's more than I can remember
JUDGE:
    Did you ever pass through the camp gate
1ST WITNESS:
    It's possible
    I remember a band
    playing there once
JUDGE:
    Were you never in the yard of Barrack 11
1ST WITNESS:
    Once perhaps
    There was said to be a wall there
    I can't remember it though
JUDGE:
    But surely a black wall
    is very noticeable
1ST WITNESS:
    I have no recollection of it
JUDGE:
    You were
    the presiding officer
    at these summary sessions
    Did the defendant have counsel
1ST WITNESS:
    If it was requested
JUDGE:
    Was it ever requested
1ST WITNESS:
    Rarely
JUDGE:
    And when it was

166

1ST WITNESS:
    Then counsel was provided
JUDGE:
    Who was the defense
1ST WITNESS:
    Somebody from the office staff
JUDGE:
    Were intensive interrogations
    ever employed
1ST WITNESS:
    There was never any need for that
    At least I personally never
    heard of any such interrogations
    The facts of the case were so clear
    there was no need
    for intensive interrogation
JUDGE:
    What were the facts of the case
1ST WITNESS:
    They were exclusively
    cases of treasonable activity
JUDGE:
    Did the prisoners confess
1ST WITNESS:
    There was nothing to deny
JUDGE:
    How were these confessions obtained
1ST WITNESS:
    By means of interrogations
JUDGE:
    Who conducted the interrogations
1ST WITNESS:
    The Political Division
JUDGE:
    As a judge
    were you ever troubled

about how these confessions
were obtained

1st Witness:

What can I do
if one or another of my people
exceeds his authority
I strictly and repeatedly
enjoined my assistants
that they were to conduct
themselves correctly
at all hearings

Judge:

Were witnesses called at interrogations

1st Witness:

Not as a rule
We asked if everything was as stated
and they all said yes

Judge:

Then you only had to deliver death sentences

1st Witness:

Yes
There were practically no acquittals
Proceedings were instituted only
when everything was perfectly clear

Judge:

Did you ever notice
any marks on the accused
which might have indicated improper treatment

1st Witness:

No

Judge:

Were women and children
executed at the Black Wall

1st Witness:

I know nothing about that

6TH WITNESS:

 Among the prisoners
 brought into the barrack
 to be sentenced by the court
 there were many women and children
 The indictment was for smuggling
 or for contact with partisan groups
 In contrast to the camp prisoners
 who were locked up in the basement
 prisoners arrested by the Security Police
 were held on the ground floor of Barrack 11
 They were taken into the session room
 one by one
 The judge read the sentence
 He only read out the names and then said
 You have been sentenced to death
 Most of the prisoners sentenced
 didn't understand the language
 and had no idea
 why they had been arrested
 From the courtroom
 they were immediately taken
 to the washroom
 where they were told to undress
 and from there
 out to the courtyard

PROSECUTING ATTORNEY:

 As judge of the summary court
 how many sentences were you
 called upon to deliver

1ST WITNESS:

 I cannot remember that

PROSECUTING ATTORNEY:

 How often
 were your sessions held

1st Witness:

I can't recall

Prosecuting Attorney:

How long
did a session of the summary court last

1st Witness:

I couldn't say

Prosecuting Attorney:

You are at present the director
of a large business concern
As such you must certainly be accustomed
to dealing with large numbers
and complex time calculations
How many people
did you sentence

1st Witness:

I don't know

6th Witness:

At a single session of the summary court
an average of 100 to 150 death sentences
was delivered
The session lasted
an hour and a half to two hours
and took place every two weeks

Prosecuting Attorney:

How many prisoners
all told
would the witness estimate
were shot at the Black Wall

6th Witness:

The death books and our own notes
show
that together
with the usual Bunker clearings
approximately 20,000 people
were shot at the Black Wall

THE SONG OF THE BLACK WALL

II

7TH WITNESS:
Early one morning
in the fall of 1943
I saw a little girl
in the courtyard of Barrack 11
She wore a red dress
and her hair was braided into a long pigtail
She stood alone
her hands at her sides
like a soldier
She bent over once
to dust her shoes off
and then stood still again
Then I saw Boger come into the courtyard
He kept his gun
hidden behind his back
He took the child by the hand
and she went along with him like a good girl
and let him stand her
face to the wall
against the Black Wall
The child looked around once more
Boger turned her face to the wall
lifted his gun
and shot her

COUNSEL FOR THE DEFENSE:
How could the witness have seen this

7TH WITNESS:

I was cleaning the washroom
which was next to the door
leading out to the yard

JUDGE:

How old was the child

7TH WITNESS:

Six or seven years old
The corpse-bearers told me later
that the girl's parents
had been shot there a few days before

ACCUSED #2:

Your Honor
I never shot a child
I never shot anyone at all

3RD WITNESS:

I saw Boger by the Black Wall many times
I can still hear him yelling
Head up
and then shooting the prisoner in the neck

JUDGE:

Isn't it possible that the witness
may be confusing Boger with someone else

3RD WITNESS:

We all knew Boger
and the way he waddled when he walked
We used to see him frequently
riding to Barrack 11 on his bicycle
his gun slung over his shoulder
Sometimes he used to pull prisoners
along behind him
like dogs on a leash

JUDGE:

Accused Boger
would you care to reconsider

your statement
that you never fired a shot in the camp

ACCUSED #2:

I stand by my statement today
and a thousand years from now
I will still stand by it
Not that I would have been afraid to shoot
I would only have been carrying out orders

3RD WITNESS:

Executions were carried out
every Wednesday and Friday
On May 14 1943
I saw Boger
kill 17 prisoners
I made a note of the date
because my friend Berger was one of them
He had already been beaten to a pulp
on the swing
Berger shouted
You murderers you criminals
then Boger shot him
Another prisoner was on his knees
in front of Boger
Boger shot him in the face
When word passed around
Boger's here
we knew what it meant
We called him
the Black Death

ACCUSED #2:

I've had a lot of nicknames besides that one
We all had nicknames
That doesn't prove anything

JUDGE:

Accused Boger
during the course of this trial

witnesses have repeatedly testified
that you
killed people in the camp
Has all this testimony
in your opinion
simply been invented

ACCUSED #2:

I was frequently
present at executions
Most likely
the witnesses are confusing me
with somebody else
They've got Boger
so what do they do
It's natural
They dump all their hate on me

JUDGE:

You didn't shoot once

ACCUSED #2:

I did
once

JUDGE:

You did shoot once

ACCUSED #2:

It was an exception
I was ordered
to take part in an execution

JUDGE:

How did that happen

ACCUSED #2:

At one of the Bunker clearings
Grabner called out the order
Sergeant Boger
will carry on with the shooting

JUDGE:

How many times did you shoot

ACCUSED #2:
>   Twice
>   on that one single occasion
>   Later I refused
>   to take part in such things
>   I said
>   Either I work here
>   or I work with Identification
>   I can't
>   do both jobs at the same time

JUDGE:
>   Who were the people
>   you had to shoot

ACCUSED #2:
>   They belonged to a transport
>   that hadn't been processed
>   by Identification

JUDGE:
>   That means
>   it was assumed from the start
>   they were going to die

ACCUSED #2:
>   I believe so

JUDGE:
>   Accused Boger
>   why have you consistently maintained
>   up until this very moment
>   that no one in the camp
>   met his death at your hand

ACCUSED #2:
>   Your Honor
>   when you get so much thrown at you
>   you just can't commit yourself right off

JUDGE:
>   And you persist in maintaining
>   that you shot in only two cases

and that no one ever died
as a result
of intensive interrogations

ACCUSED #2:

Yes
On my sacred word of honor

JUDGE:

As one of the corpse-bearers' detail
when were you required to appear
in the courtyard of Barrack 11

3RD WITNESS:

We were called up
about an hour before the execution

JUDGE:

Where were you stationed

3RD WITNESS:

In the Ambulance Barrack

JUDGE:

Where was that

3RD WITNESS:

Across from the Bunker Barrack
on the front right side of the camp

JUDGE:

How were you alerted for duty

3RD WITNESS:

A clerk ran in from Barrack 11
He shouted
Corpse-bearers
one stretcher
two stretchers
If he called for one stretcher we knew
it would be a small execution
If he called for more
it was a big one

JUDGE:

Where did the clerk stand

3RD WITNESS:

> He stayed out in the corridor
> and we ran out to him
> When he told us
> how many were needed
> the Kapo
> picked out the ones to go

JUDGE:

> Where did you have to go then

3RD WITNESS:

> When the siren had signaled the curfew
> we went out into the courtyard
> through the door in Barrack 11
> We had to line up next to the door
> and stand there with our stretchers ready

JUDGE:

> What sort of stretchers were they

3RD WITNESS:

> Canvas
> with wood shafts
> and metal legs

JUDGE:

> Was a doctor present

3RD WITNESS:

> Only for big executions
> Otherwise just the officers
> of the Political Division

JUDGE:

> Where were prisoners awaiting execution kept

3RD WITNESS:

> They were held in the washroom
> and in the hall outside

JUDGE:

> What preparations preceded the execution

3RD WITNESS:

> After prisoners came up from the cellar

they had to take off their clothes
in the washroom
or out in the hall
Numbers were written on their chests
with indelible pencil
A prisoner clerk checked out the numbers
then crossed them out
as prisoners
were taken out to the yard

JUDGE:

What order was given
to bring out the prisoners

3RD WITNESS:

The order was
Take off
Then the Bunker-Jakob ran out
with the first two
As soon as they stood against the wall
we too got the order
Take off
and we ran out with our stretcher

JUDGE:

Who gave the order

3RD WITNESS:

Either the doctor
or one of the officers

JUDGE:

Had the prisoners already been shot
when you got there

3RD WITNESS:

Usually the first one had fallen
and the second fell right after
But sometimes it took longer
Then we stood behind
the executioner

JUDGE:

Why did it sometimes take longer

3RD WITNESS:

Occasionally a gun jammed
And we'd wait while the man
took care of it

JUDGE:

How did the prisoners
who were to be executed behave

3RD WITNESS:

Some prayed
others sang national
or religious songs
Once though
when a woman started to scream
I heard the order
Get that crazy one first

JUDGE:

How did you remove the dead

3RD WITNESS:

As soon as they had dropped in the sand
in front of the wall
we picked them up by the hands and feet
laid the first one face up on the stretcher
the second one face down and reversed
so he lay with his face
between the legs of the one underneath
Then we ran to the drainage ditch
and tipped them out

JUDGE:

Where was this ditch

3RD WITNESS:

Along the left edge of the courtyard

JUDGE:

What happened then

3RD WITNESS:
>   While we ran with the stretcher
>   over to the ditch
>   the Bunker-Jakob was already running
>   the next two
>   out to the wall
>   and the two other bearers ran
>   behind him with their stretcher
>   We laid the dead down in layers
>   on top of each other
>   with their heads over the ditch
>   so the blood could drain off

JUDGE:
>   Did the prisoners die
>   immediately after execution

3RD WITNESS:
>   Sometimes the bullet
>   only went in through an ear
>   or through the chin
>   and they were still alive
>   when they were carried off
>   Then we had to put the stretcher down
>   and the injured would be shot again
>   this time in the head
>   The Arrest Supervisor Schlage
>   always took another look
>   at the bodies we had dumped
>   and if any of them still moved
>   he had him pulled out of the heap
>   and finished off the kill
>   Once Schlage said to one
>   who was still living
>   Get up
>   I saw
>   the man try to pull himself up
>   Then Schlage said

Stay down
and shot him in the heart
and in both temples
But the man was still alive
I don't know how many more he got
First
one in the throat
The blood that came out was black
Schlage said
That one has as many lives as a cat
JUDGE:
Accused Schlage
have you anything to say to this
ACCUSED #14:
It's a riddle to me
To that
I wouldn't know what to say

THE SONG OF THE BLACK WALL

III

7TH WITNESS:
> I saw Schlage in the washroom once
> with a family that had been brought in
> The father had to get down and duck-walk
> and then Schlage shot him in the head
> Then it was the child's turn
> and after that the mother
> He had to shoot the child more than once
> It screamed and didn't die right away

COUNSEL FOR THE DEFENSE:
> Why did he shoot them in the washroom
> when the Execution Wall
> was just outside

7TH WITNESS:
> Smaller executions
> were often carried out in the washroom
> because it was simpler
> The showers could be turned on
> to wash the blood off the floor

COUNSEL FOR THE DEFENSE:
> Describe the washroom

7TH WITNESS:
> It was a small room with one window
> that was covered over with a blanket
> The bottom half of the room was tarred
> the upper half painted white
> There were thick black pipes in the corners

About six feet up
a pipe with shower heads
crossed through the middle of the room
JUDGE:
Accused Schlage
do you still maintain
that you shot nobody in the camp
ACCUSED #14:
I emphatically deny
these accusations
I never took part in any killings
7TH WITNESS:
Some of the corpses
brought into the washroom
had flesh cut out of them
JUDGE:
What do you mean by that
7TH WITNESS:
In the summer of 1944
I saw the first of those mutilated corpses
A man was unloaded
whom I had already noticed
when he stripped for execution
He was a giant
I saw him lying in the washroom
There were men in white coats
and with surgical instruments
standing around him
Flesh had been cut out of his stomach
At first we thought
he must have swallowed something
and they were getting it out
but later on it happened more often
that flesh was cut out of corpses
Afterwards it was mainly the case
with bodies of the stronger heavier women

3RD WITNESS:

Once we had to remove
the corpses of 70 women
Their breasts were gone
and there were deep cuts
in their abdomens and thighs
The medical orderlies loaded
potfuls of human flesh
into the sidecar of a motorcycle
On the wagon
we had to cover up
the corpses with boards

4TH WITNESS:

In Experimental Research Barrack 10
I looked through a crack in the window
  boards
I saw the corpses down in the courtyard
We had heard a loud hum
It was swarms of flies
The ground was covered with blood
Then I saw
the executioners walking across the courtyard
smoking and laughing
    [*Points at the Accused*]

COUNSEL FOR THE DEFENSE:

We cannot allow
these insults to our clients
to pass unchallenged
We want the record
to show our objection
    [*The Accused express their indignation*]

THE SONG OF PHENOL

I

8TH WITNESS:
    I charge Medical Orderly Klehr
    with the singlehanded killing
    of thousands of prisoners
    by injecting phenol into the heart
ACCUSED #9:
    That is slander
    Only in a very few cases
    was I compelled to supervise injections
    and then
    only with the greatest reluctance
8TH WITNESS:
    At least 30 prisoners were killed
    daily in the infirmary
    Sometimes as many as 200
JUDGE:
    Where were these injections given
8TH WITNESS:
    In the Contagious Diseases Barrack nearby
    That was Barrack 20
JUDGE:
    Where was Barrack 20
8TH WITNESS:
    It was the next to the last building
    on the right-hand side
    of the center barrack row
    The last building in that row was 21
    the camp infirmary

As a prisoner attendant I had to
take selected prisoners
across the yard
to the Contagious Diseases Barrack

JUDGE:
Was this yard closed off

8TH WITNESS:
Only by low iron railings at each end

JUDGE:
How were the prisoners transferred

8TH WITNESS:
Those able to walk
crossed the courtyard half naked
They held their blanket and wooden shoes
over their heads
Many patients had to be supported
or carried over
They entered Barrack 20
through the side door

JUDGE:
In which room
were the injections given

8TH WITNESS:
In Room 1
That was the doctor's office
It was at the end of the central corridor

JUDGE:
Where did the prisoners wait

8TH WITNESS:
They had to line up in the corridor
The critically ill lay on the floor
Prisoners went into the room two by two
Dr Entress assigned Klehr
a third of the patients
That wasn't enough for him

When Dr Entress had left for the day
Klehr stayed to make additional selections

JUDGE:

You saw this yourself

8TH WITNESS:

Yes
I saw it
Klehr loved round numbers
If the final count didn't satisfy him
he went through the wards
selecting victims to round off the number
He looked over the fever charts
which under his supervision
were meticulously kept
then made his selections accordingly

JUDGE:

What were the round numbers
that Klehr especially favored

8TH WITNESS:

From about 23 on
he would round it off to 30
from 36 to 40
and so on
He ordered selected patients
to get up and follow him

JUDGE:

What order was given

8TH WITNESS:

You come along
you come along
you come along
and you

ACCUSED #9:

Your Honor
this statement is untrue
I was not authorized to make selections

JUDGE:
>   What were your duties then

ACCUSED #9:
>   I only had to see to it
>   that the right prisoners were brought over

JUDGE:
>   And what did you
>   have to do when injections were given

ACCUSED #9:
>   That's something I'd like to know myself
>   I just stood around
>   The treatment
>   was carried out by special-duty prisoners
>   I kept away from that
>   I wasn't going to let those
>   contaminated prisoners
>   breathe in my face

JUDGE:
>   As staff orderly
>   what were your duties

ACCUSED #9:
>   I was responsible
>   (a) for discipline and sanitation
>   (b) for registration
>   (c) for the patients' nutrition

JUDGE:
>   What was their diet

ACCUSED #9:
>   In the dietetic kitchen milk-soup was
>   prepared for post-operational patients

JUDGE:
>   How many patients were in the infirmary

ACCUSED #9:
>   On the average some
>   500 to 600 patients

JUDGE:

What were the accommodations

ACCUSED #9:

They lay on triple-decker bunks

JUDGE:

How were they registered

ACCUSED #9:

Every sick-report received
was card-indexed
Selections among advanced patients
were then registered

JUDGE:

What were advanced patients

ACCUSED #9:

Prisoners
whose state of health was critical

JUDGE:

How were the selections made

ACCUSED #9:

The camp doctor examined the prisoner
and the index card with the diagnosis
If he did not return the card
to the prisoner doctor
but gave it to the prisoner clerk instead
it meant
the prisoner was to receive the injection

JUDGE:

What happened then

ACCUSED #9:

The cards were assembled on a table
and processed

JUDGE:

What does processed mean

ACCUSED #9:

The prisoner clerk had
to compile a list from the cards on hand

This list was then handed over
to the medical orderly
In accordance with this list
patients were dispatched

9TH WITNESS:

On Christmas 1942
Klehr walked into the ward
and said
Today
I am camp doctor
Today
I shall take care
of the advanced patients
With the stem of his pipe
he pointed out 40 of them
and designated them for injection
After Christmas
a requisition for special rations
was put in
for Medical Orderly Klehr
I saw the requisition
It said
For Special Treatment
carried out 24 12 1942
a half-pint brandy
5 cigarettes 3½ ounces sausage
is requested

ACCUSED #9:

That's ridiculous
I had home leave every Christmas
My wife can testify to that

JUDGE:

Accused Klehr
do you still maintain
you had no part whatsoever

in selections and killings
by means of phenol injection

ACCUSED #9:

All I had to do
was supervise standard operating procedures

JUDGE:

Did you always find
these procedures justified

ACCUSED #9:

In the beginning I was astonished
when I heard
that patients were injected
by special-duty prisoners
But then I realized
that the patients were incurable
and endangered the health of the entire camp

JUDGE:

How were the injections given

ACCUSED #9:

Special-duty prisoner Peter Werl
from the Ambulance Barrack
and another called Felix
administered the injections
At first
they were injected into a vein in the arm
However due to the undernourished
condition of the prisoners
these veins were hard to find
For that reason phenol was later on
injected directly into the heart
The hypo wasn't even empty
the man was already dead

JUDGE:

Did you ever refuse
to be present at these sessions

ACCUSED #9:

    I would have been put up against the wall

JUDGE:

    You never expressed your misgivings
    to the camp doctor

ACCUSED #9:

    I did
    a number of times
    But all I was told was
    I had my duty to do

JUDGE:

    Couldn't you have arranged
    for a transfer to some other post

ACCUSED #9:

    Mr President
    we were all in a strait jacket
    We were nothing but numbers
    just like the prisoners
    With us
    a man began to count for something
    only when he had a degree
    We should have just dared try
    to question anything

JUDGE:

    Were you never compelled
    to give an injection yourself

ACCUSED #9:

    Once when I started to complain
    the camp doctor said
    In the future you'll do it yourself

JUDGE:

    And then you did undertake
    selections and killings

ACCUSED #9:

    In a few cases

yes
I was compelled to
JUDGE:
How often did you give injections
ACCUSED #9:
Generally twice a week
to about 12 to 15 men
But I was only there for two or three months
JUDGE:
That would come to at least
200 killed
ACCUSED #9:
It could have been 250 to 300
I don't remember exactly
It was orders
There wasn't anything I could do about it
8TH WITNESS:
Medical Orderly Klehr
participated
in the killing
of at least 16,000 prisoners
ACCUSED #9:
That's preposterous
I'm supposed to have injected away
16,000 people
when there were only 16,000
in the whole camp
That wouldn't have left anybody but the band
        [*The Accused laugh*]

THE SONG OF PHENOL

II

JUDGE:
  Accused Klehr
  how did you kill the prisoners
ACCUSED #9:
  As prescribed by orders
  with an injection of phenol in the heart
  But I didn't do that all by myself
JUDGE:
  Who else was there
ACCUSED #9:
  I don't remember
9TH WITNESS:
  The accused Scherpe and Hantl
  assisted in the killings by phenol
  Yet their behavior was very different
  from Klehr's
  They were polite to us
  and said Good morning
  when they came into the barrack
  and when they left they said
  Good afternoon
  We often saw Klehr wild with rage
  Scherpe
  on the other hand
  was calm and courteous
  He had a pleasant way
  of treating people
  I never saw Scherpe beat

or kick anybody
Patients who came to him
often had confidence in him
and believed they were only
going to be treated for their illness

JUDGE:

As one of the prisoner doctors
in the infirmary
what can the witness tell us
about the early stages
of phenol injection

9TH WITNESS:

It was camp doctor Entress
who initiated the injections
He began by using gasoline
but that proved to be impractical
since it took three quarters of an hour
for the patient to die
A quicker means was sought
The second to be used was hydrogen
After that came phenol

JUDGE:

Whom did you see administer
these injections

9TH WITNESS:

At first Dr Entress himself
then Scherpe and Hantl
Hantle did it infrequently
We thought of him as a decent person

JUDGE:

Did you see
Klehr kill

9TH WITNESS:

I did not see it myself
Both Schwarz and Gebhard
the two prisoners who had to hold the victim

during the injection
told me about it
But we didn't waste much time discussing it
It was such an ordinary event

COUNSEL FOR THE DEFENSE:

The witness
mentions different names
in connection
with these special-duty prisoners
Weren't the prisoners named Werl and Felix

9TH WITNESS:

There were many special-duty prisoners
who had to do this job

COUNSEL FOR THE DEFENSE:

And didn't these prisoners
also do the killing

9TH WITNESS:

In the beginning they had to

COUNSEL FOR THE DEFENSE:

So the prisoners were killed
by their own people

PROSECUTING ATTORNEY:

We protest
these tactics by which the defense
seeks to blame prisoners
for actions carried out
under the threat of death

COUNSEL FOR THE DEFENSE:

The troops in the camp
were subject to the same threat

PROSECUTING ATTORNEY:

In no instance has it been proved
that anything was done
to those who refused
to take part in killings

COUNSEL FOR THE DEFENSE:
     That is easy enough to say now
     In the eyes of the law a subordinate
     can be held responsible
     only when he knows
     that the order of his superior
     involves the commission of a civil
     or military crime
     Our clients acted in good faith
     and according to the basic principle
     of unquestioning execution of their duty
     With their oath of allegiance to the death
     all submitted to the goals
     established by
     the then existing administration
     as did also
     the Department of Justice
     and the Army
PROSECUTING ATTORNEY:
     We repeat that anyone
     who recognized the criminal intent of an
          order
     had the choice
     of requesting a transfer
     We know
     why they did not have themselves transferred
     At the front
     their own lives would have been endangered
     So they stayed
     where their enemy was defenseless
JUDGE:
     The court calls as witness
     one of the former
     ranking camp doctors
     In the course of your duties

did you have anything to do with the accused
Klehr Scherpe and Hantl

2ND WITNESS:

    I did not come into contact
with these men

JUDGE:

    Weren't you their superior

2ND WITNESS:

    Their only superior there
was the camp headquarters doctor
All I did was desk work

JUDGE:

    What was your position in the medical profes-
sion
before being called up for service in the camp

2ND WITNESS:

    I was a university professor

JUDGE:

    And yet with all your professional training
you had only office work to do

2ND WITNESS:

    Occasionally I also
did some work in pathology

JUDGE:

    You selected
no prisoners for the accused Klehr

2ND WITNESS:

    I refused to do so

JUDGE:

    You were never present during selections

2ND WITNESS:

    Only to accompany the doctor on duty

PROSECUTING ATTORNEY:

    Are you aware
that those

who took part in such actions
were granted special rations

2ND WITNESS:

I find it understandable and natural
that for the hard work they had to do
the men should receive
special rations of cigarettes
and brandy
After all it was wartime
Brandy and cigarettes were hard to come by
so of course the men were after them
They saved up their coupons
and then went over with their bottle

PROSECUTING ATTORNEY:

You too

2ND WITNESS:

Yes
Everybody went over

PROSECUTING ATTORNEY:

What was your attitude
in regard to the selections

COUNSEL FOR THE DEFENSE:

We object to this question
This witness has already
served his sentence
and he cannot be tried here again

2ND WITNESS:

I consider myself
innocent even today
The only patients chosen
were those who couldn't have recovered
anyway

PROSECUTING ATTORNEY:

With your medical training
you saw no alternative

2ND WITNESS:

> Not with the way things were then
> On the front thousands of our own soldiers
> were bleeding to death
> and people were suffering
> in the bombed-out cities

PROSECUTING ATTORNEY:

> But we are talking here
> of people who
> though they had committed no crime
> were held under arrest
> and murdered
> You must have been aware of that

2ND WITNESS:

> There was nothing I could do about it
> My first day there
> the army doctor said to me
> We're in the asshole of the world here
> and we have to behave accordingly

PROSECUTING ATTORNEY:

> Were you present
> when injections were given

2ND WITNESS:

> Yes
> I had to go in there occasionally

PROSECUTING ATTORNEY:

> What did you see there

2ND WITNESS:

> Klehr put on a doctor's coat
> and said to a girl
> You have heart trouble
> You have to have an injection
> Then he jabbed it in
> and I ran out

PROSECUTING ATTORNEY:

> Was Klehr alone

2ND WITNESS:
    Yes
PROSECUTING ATTORNEY:
    Wasn't the woman held down
2ND WITNESS:
    No
PROSECUTING ATTORNEY:
    The court is in possession of the diary
    you kept during your time in the camp
    In this diary we read
    For lunch today
    roast hare
    a thick leg of mutton
    with potato dumplings and cabbage
    It goes on to say
    Six women injected by Klehr
2ND WITNESS:
    I must have heard that somewhere
PROSECUTING ATTORNEY:
    We read further
    Bicycle trip
    wonderful weather
    Then
    Present at 11 executions
    Three women begged for their lives
    Fresh samples taken from liver
    spleen and pancreas
    following injections of pilocarpin
    What does that mean
2ND WITNESS:
    I had orders
    to perform autopsies
    The purpose of this work
    was purely scientific
    I had nothing to do with the killings

PROSECUTING ATTORNEY:
 The people whose flesh you took
 had you picked them for autopsy
 while they were still alive
COUNSEL FOR THE DEFENSE:
 We object
 and remind the prosecution once again
 that this witness has already
 paid his penalty
PROSECUTING ATTORNEY:
 Why did you use human flesh
 for your research
2ND WITNESS:
 Because the guards
 ate the beef and horse meat
 received
 for use in our bacteriological research
JUDGE:
 Where was the phenol
 used for injections
 stored
3RD WITNESS:
 It was stored in the dispensary
JUDGE:
 Where was the dispensary
3RD WITNESS:
 In the maintenance buildings outside the
 camp
JUDGE:
 Who was in charge of the dispensary
3RD WITNESS:
 Dr Capesius
JUDGE:
 Who came for the phenol
3RD WITNESS:
 The requisition

written up by Klehr
was handed over
to Dr Capesius in the dispensary
by a messenger from the infirmary
The messenger was then given the phenol

JUDGE:

Accused Dr Capesius
what do you have to say to this

ACCUSED #3:

I don't know anything
about such requisitions

JUDGE:

Did you know that people in the camp
were killed by injections of phenol

ACCUSED #3:

I heard about it for the first time
just now

JUDGE:

Did you store phenol in your dispensary

ACCUSED #3:

I never saw any great amount of it there

3RD WITNESS:

The phenol was stored in a yellow cupboard
in the corner of the prescription room
Later on there were also big bottles of it
in the cellar

COUNSEL FOR THE DEFENSE:

How does the witness
happen to know this

3RD WITNESS:

I was assigned to duty in the dispensary
I saw the new requisition forms
They had been filled out
and signed by Dr Capesius
They called it purified phenol

But I'm not sure whether
the words PRO INJECTIONE were on the forms
    too or not
JUDGE:
What quantities were requisitioned
3RD WITNESS:
Smalls amounts at first
Later
from 4½ to 11 pounds a month
JUDGE:
How is phenol
generally used as a medication
3RD WITNESS:
Mixed with glycerine
it is used for ear drops
ACCUSED #3:
That's precisely what the phenol in my keep-
    ing
was intended for
JUDGE:
4½ to 11 pounds of phenol per month
16 ounces per pound
each ounce containing hundreds of drops
You could have cured the ears
of an entire army
        [*The Accused laugh*]
Accused Capesius
do you still maintain
that in your dispensary you never saw
phenol for injection
ACCUSED #3:
I neither saw large quantities
of phenol
nor knew
that people were being killed with it

JUDGE:
> Who received the phenol
> obtained from the dispensary

3RD WITNESS:
> The doctor on duty
> He then passed it on to the orderly
> in the doctor's office

THE SONG OF PHENOL

III

JUDGE:
>   Describe the doctor's office
6TH WITNESS:
>   It was painted white
>   The windows on the courtyard side
>   were whitewashed over
JUDGE:
>   How was the room furnished
6TH WITNESS:
>   There were a few cupboards and closets
>   and then there was the curtain
>   that divided the room
JUDGE:
>   What sort of curtain was it
6TH WITNESS:
>   It was about six feet long
>   and it hung from a little below the ceiling
>   It was greenish-gray
>   The clerk who sat in front of it
>   crossed off the patients
>   as they were brought in
JUDGE:
>   What was behind the curtain
6TH WITNESS:
>   A small table
>   and a couple of stools
>   On the wall
>   there were rubber aprons

and pink rubber gloves
hanging on hooks

COUNSEL FOR THE DEFENSE:

How does the witness
know this

6TH WITNESS:

I was a corpse-bearer
We sat in the washroom right next
to the doctor's room
The door was open
and we could see everything

JUDGE:

What happened to the prisoners
who were to be given
the phenol injection

6TH WITNESS:

They were brought in two at a time
from the corridor
One of the two special-duty prisoners
who stood ready behind the curtain
held one prisoner
while the injection was given
The other one had to wait
on the other side of the curtain
Meanwhile the second special-duty prisoner
had filled the hypodermic

JUDGE:

What kind of syringe was used

6TH WITNESS:

At first
when they gave intravenous injections
they were syringes with a capacity of five cc's
Later
when injections were made
directly into the heart
they used syringes that held only two cc's

They were fitted with needles
generally used for making lumbar punctures
A supply of syringes was kept in a pouch

JUDGE:

In what sort of vessel was
the phenol kept

6TH WITNESS:

In a bottle
similar to a thermos
The phenol was poured out
into a small basin
The syringes were filled from this
The fluid turned red
because needles were seldom changed
and they were bloody from the injections

JUDGE:

Did the patients know
what was going to happen to them

6TH WITNESS:

Most of them did not
They were told
they were going to be inoculated

JUDGE:

They allowed
this to be done to them

6TH WITNESS:

Most of them did as they were told
Many were in a state of utter exhaustion

JUDGE:

Whom did you see administer injections

6TH WITNESS:

Klehr took the syringe
when it had been filled
He wore a rubber apron
rubber gloves and high rubber boots

The sleeves of his white coat
were rolled up

JUDGE:

What happened to the prisoner then

6TH WITNESS:

If he still had a shirt on
he had to take it off
and sit down on the stool
He had to hold his left arm up
and out to the side
and cover his mouth with his hand
That was to smother the scream
and to leave the heart open
The two special-duty prisoners
held him down

JUDGE:

What were their names

6TH WITNESS:

They were called Schwarz and Weiss
Schwarz held the prisoner
by the shoulders
Weiss kept the prisoner's hand
against his mouth
and Klehr jabbed the needle
into his heart

JUDGE:

Did death occur immediately

6TH WITNESS:

Most of them made a faint sound
as if they were exhaling
Generally they were dead then
The death rattle went on in some of them
and stopped only
after they had been taken off
to the washroom
Some were still in their death agony

when we took them off
The rest were dragged out
with a leather thong
we slipped around their wrists
It went very quickly
Often two or three patients
were finished off
inside a minute

JUDGE:

What happened to those
who were still alive
after the injection

6TH WITNESS:

I remember a man
who was tall and powerfully built
He got up to his feet in the washroom
with the injection in his heart
I remember it very clearly
There was a boiler
and next to it a bench
Holding on to the boiler
and the bench
he pulled himself up
Then Klehr came in
and gave him a second injection
Others were sometimes only unconscious
because the needle hadn't gone into the heart
and the phenol had entered the lung
When he was done for the day
Klehr always went into the washroom
to look over the stacked-up bodies
If one of them was still alive
he shot him in the back of the neck
Or sometimes he would just say
This one won't make it to the crematorium

JUDGE:

Did it ever happen that living prisoners
were taken out with the dead
6TH WITNESS:

Sometimes
yes
JUDGE:

And they were burned alive
6TH WITNESS:

Yes
Or killed with a shovel
at the ovens
JUDGE:

Did prisoners ever
resist
6TH WITNESS:

Once there was a loud shout
This is what I saw
The two special-duty prisoners
were sitting on top of a bare-chested man
who was smeared all over with blood
The man's head had been split open
A poker was lying on the floor
Klehr stood there
the hypodermic in his hand
Klehr knelt down on top of the man
who was still thrashing violently
and jabbed the needle in
JUDGE:

Accused Klehr
what do you have to say to these accusations
ACCUSED #9:

I know nothing about the case in question
JUDGE:

Do you recognize the witness

ACCUSED #9:
>   Your Honor
>   This is important
>   I don't know this witness
>   and I knew every single prisoner
>   employed in the corpse-bearer detail

7TH WITNESS:
>   On September 28 1942
>   it was my father's turn
>   He was brought in
>   together with another prisoner
>   Klehr said to him
>   You're going to be given
>   a typhus shot now
>   He quickly injected both of them
>   in the heart
>   He was in a hurry
>   to get back to his rabbit-breeding
>   I held my father
>   and then carried him out myself

JUDGE:
>   Accused Klehr
>   do you know the witness

ACCUSED #9:
>   That's Weiss
>   He was weeping at the time
>   so I asked him why he was weeping
>   Had he told me
>   right away that it was his father
>   I would have let him live

JUDGE:
>   Why didn't you tell him right away

7TH WITNESS:
>   I was scared
>   Klehr would say
>   Sit down next to him

JUDGE:

Were children among those
killed by injection

7TH WITNESS:

Once in the spring of 1943
more than 100 children were killed

JUDGE:

Who carried out this killing

7TH WITNESS:

The killing was carried out
by staff orderlies Hantl and Scherpe

JUDGE:

Can the witness
provide us with the exact number
of children killed at that time

7TH WITNESS:

There were 119 children

JUDGE:

Do you recall the exact date

7TH WITNESS:

It was the 23rd of February

JUDGE:

How do you know this

7TH WITNESS:

I was the clerk at that execution
It was my job
to cross the children off the list
They were boys from 13 to 17 years old
Their parents had been shot earlier

JUDGE:

Where did these children come from

7TH WITNESS:

They came from the province of Zamos
a region that had been cleared
to make room for settlers
from the home country

JUDGE:
>Accused Scherpe
>did you take part in this killing

ACCUSED #10:
>Mr Chairman
>I would like to state categorically
>that I never killed a single person

JUDGE:
>Accused Hantl
>what do you have to say

ACCUSED #11:
>That children were shipped in too
>is completely new to me
>Excuse me
>Mr Scherpe
>did we ever have anything to do
>with children

JUDGE:
>You are not permitted here
>to put any questions to other accused
>What we want to know from you
>is whether you took part
>in the killings by injection

ACCUSED #11:
>All I can say to that
>is that these accusations are lies

JUDGE:
>Were you present
>when the injections were given

ACCUSED #11:
>At first I refused
>I said
>Is it absolutely necessary
>for me to be around
>a mess like that

Anyway I was only there about
eight or ten times

JUDGE:

How many were killed
the times you were there

ACCUSED #11:

Not more than five to eight people
Then it was over

7TH WITNESS:

Hantl helped
select the patients
and he helped kill them
Injections were given almost daily
The only day they weren't was Sunday

ACCUSED #11:

That really makes me laugh
I never heard such nonsense in my life
I simply can't understand
why this witness
of all people
should single me out
when I was the one who helped him out
when he had committed sabotage

JUDGE:

What had he done

ACCUSED #11:

He had stolen sheets
I always did everything I could
to help the prisoners
I managed to get fuel for them
and radishes too

JUDGE:

And you did not take part in the killings

ACCUSED #11:

No
I did not

JUDGE:

    Will the witness
    resume his report
    concerning the children

7TH WITNESS:

    The children had been brought
    into the courtyard
    They played out there in the morning
    Somebody had even given them a ball
    The prisoners there
    knew what was going to happen to them
    They gave them the best of whatever they
       had
    The children were hungry and anxious
    They said they had been beaten
    They asked us over and over
    Are we going to be killed
    Scherpe and Hantl came in the afternoon
    During the hours
    in which they carried out this action
    Barrack 20 was quiet as the grave

JUDGE:

    Did the children suspect
    what was going to happen

7TH WITNESS:

    The first ones screamed
    Then they were told
    they were going to be vaccinated
    Then they went in quietly
    Only the last ones
    started to scream again
    because their friends
    hadn't come out again
    They were brought in to me
    two by two
    and then went in singly

behind the curtain
The only sound I heard
was the thump
when their heads and bodies
struck the washroom floor
Suddenly Scherpe ran out
I heard him say
I can't any more
He ran off somewhere
Hantl took care of the rest
After that
the rumor spread around camp
Scherpe's had a breakdown

JUDGE:

Accused Scherpe
do you have anything to say to this

ACCUSED #10:

The report of the witness
seems greatly exaggerated to me
Anyway
I don't recall any of this

PROSECUTING ATTORNEY:

Altogether
how many people
would the witness estimate
were killed by phenol injections

7TH WITNESS:

Going by figures in the camp books
as well as by our personal calculations
approximately 30,000 people

THE SONG OF
THE BUNKER BLOCK

I

8TH WITNESS:
    I was sentenced
    to 30 times in the standing cell
    That meant
    punitive hard labor during the day
    nights in the standing cell
JUDGE:
    Why were you sentenced
8TH WITNESS:
    I went through the food line twice
JUDGE:
    Where were the standing cells
8TH WITNESS:
    At the end of the cellar corridor
    in Barrack 11
    There were four of them
JUDGE:
    How large was a cell
8TH WITNESS:
    Three feet square
    and about six feet high
JUDGE:
    Was there a window
8TH WITNESS:
    No
    There was an air hole up in the corner

218

an inch and a half square
The air shaft went out through the wall
It was closed up on the outside
with a perforated tin lid

JUDGE:

And the door

8TH WITNESS:

You had to crawl in at the bottom
through a wooden hatchway
about 20 inches high
Outside was an iron gate
that bolted shut

JUDGE:

Were you alone in the cell

8TH WITNESS:

At first I was alone
The last week
there were four of us standing in there

JUDGE:

Were prisoners
there
day and night

8TH WITNESS:

That was the usual sentence
The method varied
Some prisoners were fed only
every two or three days
Others weren't fed at all
Those had been sentenced to death
by starvation
My friend Kurt Pachala
died in the adjoining cell
after 15 days
Toward the end he ate his shoes
He died the 14th of January 1943
I remember that

because it was my birthday
A prisoner sentenced to
the standing cell without food
could scream and swear
as much as he wanted
The door was never opened
For the first five nights
he screamed
Then hunger stopped
and thirst took over
He begged
he prayed and he moaned
He drank his urine
and licked the walls
The thirst went on for 13 days
Then no sound came from his cell
It took more than two weeks
for him to die
Corpses had to be scraped
out of the standing cells
with iron rods

JUDGE:

Why
had this man been sentenced

8TH WITNESS:

He had tried to escape
Before he was put in the cell
he had to march past
the prisoners
lined up for evening roll call
He had a sign tied to him
that read
HURRAY I'M BACK AGAIN
While he shouted out the words on the sign
he had to beat on a drum
Of those sentenced to the standing cell

Bruno Graf was the prisoner
who lasted the longest
Arrest Supervisor Schlage
used to stand at this door sometimes
when Graf was bellowing in there
and I heard Schlage
yell
Why don't you just die
It took Graf a month to die

JUDGE:

Accused Schlage
did you allow prisoners to starve to death
in the standing cells

ACCUSED #14:

Mr Chairman
I request permission to say the following
I was
if I may say so
only the lock-up man
I received my orders from my superiors
and I was duty-bound to carry them out
For what took place in the Bunker
I was not responsible
The Chief Arrest Supervisor was responsible

JUDGE:

Who brought food to the prisoners

ACCUSED #14:

Special-duty prisoners did that

JUDGE:

Who locked the cells

ACCUSED #14:

Special-duty prisoners did that too
We Arrest Supervisors
were only responsible
for unlocking the outside gates
when the Political Division arrived

JUDGE:

    Did prisoners

    die in the Arrest Bunker

ACCUSED #14:

    That's possible

    But I can't really remember

JUDGE:

    Who kept the Death Book

    and entered causes of death

ACCUSED #14:

    Only special-duty prisoners did all that

JUDGE:

    And you had nothing to do

ACCUSED #14:

    I had our own people to guard

    There were sometimes as many

    as 18 of them

    I had to make

    sure

    they didn't try to kill themselves

    or do some other dumb thing

JUDGE:

    You mean to say

    that members of units serving in the camp

    were also jailed in the Bunker

ACCUSED #14:

    Of course

    There was justice for all

    Surely Your Honor

    every sign of weakness

    had to be fought against

THE SONG OF
THE BUNKER BLOCK

II

JUDGE:
   How large were the other cells
   in the Bunker
9TH WITNESS:
   The other cells were roughly
   eight feet wide
   eight feet long
   eight feet high
   Some were dark cells
   The rest had a small window
   with a concrete rim
   The only air vent was
   high up in the wall
   It was an opening no bigger
   than the palm of your hand
JUDGE:
   How many such cells were there
9TH WITNESS:
   28 cells
JUDGE:
   How many prisoners
   could be put in a cell
9TH WITNESS:
   In that space
   there were often as many
   as 40 prisoners

JUDGE:

How long did they have to stay there

9TH WITNESS:

Often for several weeks
The prisoner Bogdan Glinski
was in there for more than 17 weeks
from November 13 1942
till March 9 1943

JUDGE:

How was the cell furnished

9TH WITNESS:

There was only a wooden box
with a bucket in it

JUDGE:

What regulations applied
to prisoners put in these cells

9TH WITNESS:

Here too the sentence was either
overnight confinement
or long-term confinement
And here too confinement
without food was practiced

JUDGE:

Which punishment did you undergo

9TH WITNESS:

I spent two nights in there

JUDGE:

Would you describe what happened

9TH WITNESS:

I had to report at Barrack 11
at 9 o'clock at night
together with 38 other prisoners
The Barrack-elder reported
the count
to the Barrack-leader on duty
Then he took us down to the basement

and locked us into Cell 20
By 10 o'clock
the air was already stifling
We stood crowded against each other
We couldn't sit down
and we couldn't lie down
It was soon so hot
we started taking off our jackets
and pants
Around midnight
we couldn't stand any more
Some collapsed
The others hung on to each other
Most of the prisoners were tense
and restless
and shoved and swore
at each other
The smell
from the men who were suffocating
mixed with the stink
coming out of the bucket
The weak got trampled
The stronger fought
to get up next to the door
where a little air came in
We shouted and pounded on the door
we battered and hammered at it
but it didn't give
Once in a while
the peep hole was opened outside
and the jailer on duty
looked in at us
By 2 o'clock in the morning
most of the prisoners
had lost consciousness
At 5

the door was opened
We were pulled out
into the corridor
We were all naked
Of the 38 who went in
19 were still alive
Of these 19
6 were taken to the infirmary
where 4 died

3RD WITNESS:

I belonged to the corpse detail
that had to clean out the hunger cells
Frequently
the dead in there had bites
in their buttocks and thighs
Often those
who had held out the longest
had some fingers missing
I asked the Bunker-Jakob
who was in charge of cleaning the Bunker
How can you stand it
He said
Praise be
what makes a man hard
Everything's fine with me
I eat their rations
Their death doesn't move me
All this moves me about as much
as that stone in the wall

THE SONG OF
THE BUNKER BLOCK

III

6TH WITNESS:
On the 3rd of September 1941
the first experiments
in mass killings
using the gas Cyklon B
were carried out in the Bunker
Staff medical orderlies and guards
brought about 850 Soviet prisoners of war
and 220 prisoner patients
to Barrack 11
After they had been locked in the cells
earth was shoveled against the windows
to seal them off
Then the gas
was funneled in
through the air holes
The next day it was ascertained
that some of the prisoners
were still alive
As a result
another portion of Cyklon B
was poured in
On the 5th of September
I was ordered to report to Barrack 11
together with 20 prisoners
from the penal company

We were told
that we were being sent
on a special work assignment
and that the penalty
for revealing what we saw there
was death
We were also promised extra rations
when the work was done
We were issued gas masks
and had to get
the corpses out of the cells
When we opened the doors
the tight pack of people
fell out against us
Even dead they were still standing
Their faces were blue
Many of them had bunches of hair
in their hands
It took us the whole day
to pry them apart
and stack them in the courtyard
That evening the commanding officer
and his staff
came
I heard the commanding officer say
Now I'm relieved
Now that we have this gas
we'll be spared all those bloodbaths
The victims too
will be spared
until the very last moment

THE SONG OF CYKLON B

I

3RD WITNESS:
> In the summer and fall of 1941
> I worked in the camp's laundry room
> That's where dirty laundry was taken
> to be fumigated with the gas Cyklon B
> Our superior was
> the fumigator Breitwieser

JUDGE:
> Does the witness
> see this person
> in this room

3RD WITNESS:
> That is Breitwieser
>> [*Accused #17 nods to the witness agreeably*]
>
> On September 3rd
> I saw Breitwieser
> accompanied by Stark
> and some other officers
> from the Political Division
> walking to Barrack 11
> with gas masks and cans
> Then the curfew sounded
> The next morning
> Breitwieser was in a bad mood
> because something had gone wrong
> The place hadn't been sealed off properly
> and the gassing

had to be repeated
Two days later
trucks loaded with corpses
drove off from the courtyard

JUDGE:

What time was it when you saw Breitwieser
on his way to Barrack 11
on September 3rd

3RD WITNESS:

About 9 o'clock at night

ACCUSED #17:

That's impossible
In the first place
I was never in the camp at night
Secondly nobody
could possibly have recognized me
at that time of the year
since a heavy fog
always came up from the river around then

JUDGE:

Did you know
that prisoners were to be gassed
in Barrack 11 that night

ACCUSED #17:

Yes
that had gotten around

JUDGE:

You did not see
prisoners being driven into the Barrack

ACCUSED #17:

Mr President
our workday was over at 6 p m
I was never in the camp after 6

JUDGE:

You never had to issue clothing

after 6 o'clock
even if new transports had arrived

ACCUSED #17:

When prisoners arrived after 6
special-duty prisoners picked up the key
to the changing room
and issued the clothes

JUDGE:

What were your duties
as fumigator

ACCUSED #17:

If I may say so
I had to give instructions

JUDGE:

Had you been trained
for this job

ACCUSED #17:

In the summer of 1941
with 10 or 15 others
I was detailed to the fumigation squad
Some men from the Degesch Company
delivered the gas
They also gave us our instructions
They taught us how to use the gas
and how to use the masks
that were equipped
with special headgear

JUDGE:

How was the gas packed

ACCUSED #17:

It came in cans
a pound each
They looked like coffee cans
At first they had gray cardboard tops
The cardboard was usually slightly moist
Later on they had metal lids

JUDGE:

What did the contents look like

ACCUSED #17:

It was a grainy crumbly substance
It's hard to describe
It looked something like starch
bluish white

JUDGE:

Do you know what this substance
was made of

ACCUSED #17:

Hydrocyanic acid
in its chemically bonded form
As soon as the crystals
were exposed to the air
cyanide gas was produced

JUDGE:

What did your work with the gas involve

ACCUSED #17:

Prisoners had to hang up their clothes
in the changing room
Then I and an assistant threw in the gas
After 24 hours the clothes
were taken out
and new ones brought in
and so on
We also had to fumigate living quarters
After the windows had been sealed
the cans were pried open
and a rubber cover quickly slipped on
Otherwise the gas began to escape
and we still had several more cans
that had to be opened
When everything was ready
the stuff was scattered

JUDGE:

    Was any warning agent
    mixed in with the gas

ACCUSED #17:

    No
    Cyklon B worked very rapidly
    I remember
    once Corporal Theurer
    went in a house
    that had been fumigated
    During the night
    the ground floor had been aired
    and the next morning Theurer
    went upstairs to the second floor
    to open the windows
    He must have breathed in some fumes
    because he fell over immediately
    rolled down the stairs unconscious
    and right on out
    to where he got some fresh air
    If he had fallen any other way
    he never would have gotten out of there

PROSECUTING ATTORNEY:

    With your professional experience
    were you not called in as an adviser
    when Cyklon B began to be used
    on prisoners

ACCUSED #17:

    I speak nothing but the truth
    as a matter of principle
    I could not stand the gas
    It gave me indigestion
    I applied for transfer

PROSECUTING ATTORNEY:

    Were you transferred

ACCUSED #17:
    Not right away
PROSECUTING ATTORNEY:
    When were you transferred
ACCUSED #17:
    I don't remember that any more
PROSECUTING ATTORNEY:
    You were transferred in April 1944
    Before then you were promoted twice
    Your first promotion
    was to private first class
    then to corporal
COUNSEL FOR THE DEFENSE:
    We object
    to the prosecution's insinuations
    The fact that members of the camp staff
    were promoted
    must be judged only within the context
    of their military duty
    In no way does it prove complicity
        [*The Accused show their agreement*]

THE SONG OF CYKLON B

II

JUDGE:
>Where was the gas stored

6TH WITNESS:
>It was stored in crates
>in the dispensary basement

JUDGE:
>Accused Capesius
>as head of the dispensary
>were you aware that Cyklon B
>was stored there

ACCUSED #3:
>I believe
>the witness is the victim
>of some confusion here
>In regard to those crates in the basement
>they contained Ovaltine
>They were a shipment from the Swiss
>Red Cross

6TH WITNESS:
>I saw the cases of Ovaltine
>and I saw the crates of Cyklon
>and I also saw the suitcases
>where the accused Capesius
>kept jewelry and gold fillings

ACCUSED #3:
>This is a complete fabrication

6TH WITNESS:
>Where did the money come from

which made it possible
for the accused Capesius
to open his own pharmacy
and a beauty parlor
immediately after the war
Be beautiful
with beauty treatments by Capesius
That was his firm's advertisement

ACCUSED #3:

I obtained this money by taking out a loan

6TH WITNESS:

And where do the 12,500 dollars come from
that were offered to me
and other witnesses
if we would testify here
that Capesius
was only in charge of the dispensary
and was not in charge of
the phenol and Cyklon B

ACCUSED #3:

I don't know anything about that

PROSECUTING ATTORNEY:

Who made this attempt to bribe you

6TH WITNESS:

It came from an anonymous source

PROSECUTING ATTORNEY:

Do you know
whether any of the legal-aid societies
of the camp guards
were behind the bribe

6TH WITNESS:

I don't know
However I would like to call
to the attention of the court
this letter
which was sent to me

The heading of the letter reads
Working Committee for Justice and Freedom
The letter itself
You will soon disappear
You will die an agonizing death
Our people are keeping you
under constant observation
You can choose now
Life or death

JUDGE:

The court will take this matter
under investigation

COUNSEL FOR THE DEFENSE:

Can the witness
tell us what was printed on the crates

6TH WITNESS:

Caution
Poison gas
There was also a warning label
with a skull and crossbones

COUNSEL FOR THE DEFENSE:

Did you see what was in the crates

6TH WITNESS:

I saw opened crates
with the cans inside

COUNSEL FOR THE DEFENSE:

What was on the labels

6TH WITNESS:

Poison gas
Cyklon

COUNSEL FOR THE DEFENSE:

Was there anything else on the labels

6TH WITNESS:

Caution
Contains no warning agent
To be opened only by experienced personnel

JUDGE:
　　Did the witness
　　see these cans actually
　　being taken to the gas chambers
6TH WITNESS:
　　We had to load the crates
　　into the ambulance
　　that came around to pick it up
JUDGE:
　　Who rode in that ambulance
6TH WITNESS:
　　I saw Dr Frank and Dr Schatz
　　as well as Dr Capesius
　　They had their gas masks with them
　　Dr Schatz was wearing his steel helmet
　　I remember that
　　because somebody in the car
　　laughed and said
　　You look like a little toadstool
COUNSEL FOR THE DEFENSE:
　　We would like to remind the court
　　that at certain times during the war
　　the wearing of gas masks was mandatory
　　Neither the coming or going of our clients
　　with gas masks
　　proves anything about where they had gone
JUDGE:
　　Did the witness
　　see delivery receipts
　　for gas shipments
6TH WITNESS:
　　When these shipments arrived
　　I was often assigned
　　to take the accompanying bills
　　to the administration
　　The shipments grew increasingly large

and finally had to be stored
outside the camp in the old theater
The sender was
The Blight Prevention Company

JUDGE:

How were these shipments
forwarded to the camp

6TH WITNESS:

Some were trucked in
directly from the factory
Others came in by rail
on army bills of lading

JUDGE:

Do you recall the amounts declared

6TH WITNESS:

14 to 20 crates
came in at a time

JUDGE:

According to your calculations
how often did these shipments arrive

6TH WITNESS:

At least once a week
In 1944
several times a week
Then trucks from the motor pool
were called in to help out

JUDGE:

How many cans
were in a crate

6TH WITNESS:

Each crate held 30 one-pound cans

JUDGE:

Was the price marked

6TH WITNESS:

The price was 50 cents a pound

JUDGE:
    How many pounds
    were required for a single gassing
6TH WITNESS:
    For 2000 people in one chamber
    about 16 pounds
JUDGE:
    At 50 cents per pound
    8 dollars

THE SONG OF CYKLON B

III

JUDGE:
  Accused Mulka
  as camp adjutant
  you were in charge of the motor pool
  Did you write up
  the transportation orders
ACCUSED #1:
  I wrote no such orders
  I had nothing to do with that
JUDGE:
  Did you know the meaning of the phrase
  Requisitions for Material for Relocation
ACCUSED #1:
  No
JUDGE:
  Accused Mulka
  the court has in its possession orders
  for the transportation of Material for Reloca-
    tion
  These documents bear your signature
ACCUSED #1:
  It is possible
  that I may have had to sign
  some such order occasionally
JUDGE:
  You never found out
  that Material for Relocation
  was in fact the gas Cyklon B

ACCUSED #1:
    As I already said
    I wasn't aware of that
JUDGE:
    Who issued requisitions for this material
ACCUSED #1:
    They came in over the teletype
    and were then passed on
    to the commanding officer
    or a protective-custody camp leader
    They were sent on from there
    to the head of the motor pool
JUDGE:
    Weren't you in charge there
ACCUSED #1:
    Only in disciplinary matters
JUDGE:
    But weren't you concerned
    to know
    to what use trucks from your motor pool
    were being put
ACCUSED #1:
    I knew of course
    that they were required
    for the transport of material
JUDGE:
    Were prisoners also
    transported in these trucks
ACCUSED #1:
    I don't know anything about that
    In my time
    prisoners walked
JUDGE:
    Accused Mulka
    the court has in its possession a document
    which deals with

the urgently required completion
of the new crematoriums
It also refers to the fact that
the prisoners used for this project
were required to work on Sundays as well
The document bears your signature

ACCUSED #1:

Yes
well
I must have dictated it then

JUDGE:

Do you still maintain
you knew nothing
about the mass killings

ACCUSED #1:

All my previous statements
conform to the truth

JUDGE:

The court has summoned as witness
the former chief mechanic
of the motor-pool repair shop
Will the witness tell us
how many trucks there were
in the motor pool

1ST WITNESS:

For heavy duty
there were ten 2½-ton trucks

JUDGE:

From whom did you receive
your transportation orders

1ST WITNESS:

From the head of the motor pool

JUDGE:

Who signed the orders

1ST WITNESS:

I don't know

JUDGE:
> What were the trucks used for

1ST WITNESS:
> For picking up freight
> and transporting prisoners

JUDGE:
> Where were the prisoners taken

1ST WITNESS:
> I can't say for sure

JUDGE:
> Did you take part
> in any of these transports

1ST WITNESS:
> I had to go along once
> as a replacement

JUDGE:
> Where did you go

1ST WITNESS:
> Into the camp
> where they picked them out
> and so on

JUDGE:
> Where did you take them

1ST WITNESS:
> To the far end of the camp
> There were woods over there
> a birch wood
> That's where the people were unloaded

JUDGE:
> Where did they go

1ST WITNESS:
> Into a house
> I didn't see anything else after that

JUDGE:
> What happened to the people

1ST WITNESS:
    I don't know
    I wasn't in there
JUDGE:
    Didn't you find out
    what happened to them
1ST WITNESS:
    Well
    yes
    They were burned up
    right then and there

THE SONG OF THE FIRE OVENS

I

JUDGE:
> The witness
> drove one of the ambulances
> that carried
> Cyklon B in its solid state
> to the gas chambers

2ND WITNESS:
> I was originally assigned to the camp
> as a tractor driver
> Later on I had to drive an ambulance too

JUDGE:
> Where did you have to drive

2ND WITNESS:
> I had to pick up
> the medical orderlies and the doctors

JUDGE:
> Who were the doctors

2ND WITNESS:
> I can't remember

JUDGE:
> Where did you have to take them

2ND WITNESS:
> From the old camp
> to the arrival platform in the new camp

JUDGE:
> When

2ND WITNESS:
> When transports arrived

JUDGE:

How were transport arrivals announced

2ND WITNESS:

By a siren

JUDGE:

Where did you drive to
from the arrival platform

2ND WITNESS:

To the crematoriums

JUDGE:

Did the doctors go with you

2ND WITNESS:

Yes

JUDGE:

What did they do there

2ND WITNESS:

The doctors stayed in the ambulance
or stood around outside
The medical orderlies had to
take care of everything

JUDGE:

What did they have to take care of

2ND WITNESS:

The gassings

JUDGE:

When you got there
were the people already
in the gas chambers

2ND WITNESS:

They were still getting undressed

JUDGE:

Was there ever any trouble

2ND WITNESS:

The times I was there
things always went smoothly

JUDGE:

> What could you see
> of the gassing procedure

2ND WITNESS:

> When the prisoners had been taken
> into the chambers
> the orderlies went up to the vents
> put on their gas masks
> and emptied their cans

JUDGE:

> Where were these vents

2ND WITNESS:

> There was an embankment that went up
> and over the underground room
> It had four compartments

JUDGE:

> How many cans were emptied

2ND WITNESS:

> Three or four
> in each hole

JUDGE:

> How long did this take

2ND WITNESS:

> About a minute

JUDGE:

> Didn't the people scream

2ND WITNESS:

> When one of them realized
> what was going on
> yes
> you could hear a scream

PROSECUTING ATTORNEY:

> How far from the gas chamber
> was your ambulance parked

2ND WITNESS:

> It was on the road
> about 20 yards off

PROSECUTING ATTORNEY:

> And from there you could hear
> what was happening down in the chambers

2ND WITNESS:

> Sometimes I got out
> to wait around outside

PROSECUTING ATTORNEY:

> What did you do there

2ND WITNESS:

> Nothing
> I smoked a cigarette

PROSECUTING ATTORNEY:

> Did you ever get near the vents
> above the gas chamber

2ND WITNESS:

> Sometimes I walked up and down a bit
> to stretch my legs

PROSECUTING ATTORNEY:

> What did you hear

2ND WITNESS:

> When they took the lids off the vents
> I heard a humming from down there
> as if a lot of people were underground

PROSECUTING ATTORNEY:

> And what did you do then

2ND WITNESS:

> The vents were shut again
> and I had to drive back

JUDGE:

> You were prisoner doctor
> in the Special Commando
> assigned to duty at the crematoriums

How many prisoners
were in that Commando
7TH WITNESS:
A total of 860 men
Each Special Commando was destroyed
after a few months
and replaced by a new crew
JUDGE:
Under whom did you serve
7TH WITNESS:
Dr Mengele
JUDGE:
How did the delivery of prisoners
to the gas chambers proceed
7TH WITNESS:
A whistle from the locomotive
on its way from the platform to the gate
was the signal
that a new shipment had arrived
That meant
that inside an hour
the ovens had to be fully operational
The electric motors were switched on
These started up the fans
that brought the fire in the ovens
up to the required temperature
JUDGE:
Could you see
the groups coming off the arrival platform
7TH WITNESS:
From the window in my workroom
I could see the upper half of the platform
and the road to the crematorium
The people arrived five abreast
The sick came behind in the trucks

The crematorium area
was closed off by an iron fence
There were warnings posted at the gate
The accompanying guards had to stop there
and the Special Commando took over
Only doctors staff orderlies
and members of the Political Division
were allowed in

JUDGE:

Which of the accused
did you see there

7TH WITNESS:

I saw Stark there and Hofmann
also Kaduk and Baretzki

COUNSEL FOR THE DEFENSE:

We call attention to the fact
that our clients
deny having participated in these events

JUDGE:

Will the witness continue his account

7TH WITNESS:

The people
went through the gate slowly and wearily
Children hung on to their mother's skirts
Old men carried babies
or pushed baby carriages
The path was covered with black cinders
and on the grass on each side of the path
there were pipes with water faucets
The people crowded around them
and the Commando let them drink
but hurried them on
There was still about 60 yards to go
before they got to the stairs
that led down to the anteroom

JUDGE:

Was there an unobstructed view
of the crematorium

7TH WITNESS:

It was surrounded by bushes and trees
and was set back about 100 yards away
from the fence surrounding the area
Beyond that fence was the outer fence
with observation towers
Back of them were open fields

JUDGE:

What could be seen
of the crematorium installations

7TH WITNESS:

Only the incineration building
with its large square chimney
Underground it was connected
by a corridor
that led to the gas chambers
and branched off
to the anteroom

JUDGE:

How large was the anteroom

7TH WITNESS:

About 50 yards long
Some 12 to 15 steps led down to it
The room was over six feet high
In the middle
there was a row of supporting columns

JUDGE:

How many people were taken down at a time

7TH WITNESS:

From one to two thousand people

JUDGE:

Did they know
what lay before them

7TH WITNESS:

> At the head of the narrow staircase
> there were signs
> that said in various languages
> BATH AND DISINFECTION ROOM
> That sounded reassuring
> and calmed a lot of people
> who were still mistrustful
> I often saw people
> go down there quite happily
> and mothers joked with their children

JUDGE:

> Was there never any outbreak of panic
> with so many people
> in such a small place

7TH WITNESS:

> Everything always went quickly
> and smoothly
> The command to undress was given
> and while the people were still
> looking around bewildered
> the Special Commando began to
> help them off
> with their clothes
> There were benches along the walls
> with numbered pegs over them
> It was repeatedly announced
> that clothes and shoes
> must be hung on the peg
> and that its number
> must not be forgotten
> to avoid unnecessary confusion
> upon return from the bath
> In the glaring light of that room
> the people took off their clothes

Men and women
old and young
Children

JUDGE:

Did this great number of people
never once
attack their guards

7TH WITNESS:

Only once did I hear
somebody shout
They're going to kill us
But somebody answered
That's impossible
That can't happen
Keep calm
And when children started crying
their parents comforted them
and joked and played with them
as they carried them
into the next room

JUDGE:

Where was the entrance to that room

7TH WITNESS:

At the end of the anteroom
It was a solid oak door
with a peep hole
and a hand-wheel
that screwed the door shut

JUDGE:

How long did the undressing take

7TH WITNESS:

About 10 minutes
Then they were all shoved
into the next room

JUDGE:

Was force ever used

254

7TH WITNESS:
>   The men in the Special Commando shouted
>   Move step it up
>   the water's getting cold
>   Naturally there were also
>   threats and beatings
>   or one of the guards
>   would fire a shot

JUDGE:
>   Was this other room
>   equipped with showers
>   or disguised in any way

7TH WITNESS:
>   No
>   There was nothing

JUDGE:
>   How big was this room

7TH WITNESS:
>   Smaller than the anteroom
>   About 30 yards long

JUDGE:
>   Certainly with 1000 or more people crowded
>   into such a small space
>   there must have been some disturbance

7TH WITNESS:
>   It was too late then
>   The last ones were pushed in
>   and the door screwed shut

JUDGE:
>   Can the witness
>   offer any explanation
>   why the people permitted
>   all this to happen to them
>   Faced with that room
>   they must have known
>   they were facing death

7TH WITNESS:

> No one had ever come out
> to tell about it

JUDGE:

> Once they were in
> what did they see

7TH WITNESS:

> There were concrete walls
> and some valves on the walls
> In the middle of the room were the pillars
> and on each side two posts
> made out of perforated sheet iron
> There were drains in the floor
> This room too was brightly lit

JUDGE:

> What could be heard
> from the people in there

7TH WITNESS:

> They began to scream
> and they pounded on the door
> but you couldn't hear much
> because of the strong roar
> that came from the cremation room

JUDGE:

> What could be seen
> through the window in the door

7TH WITNESS:

> The people crowded the door
> and climbed up the pillars
> They began to suffocate
> when the gas was thrown in

THE SONG OF THE FIRE OVENS

II

7TH WITNESS:
    The gas was poured
    into the sheet-iron posts from up above
    There was a spiral channel
    inside the post
    which spread the substance
    In the moist hot air
    it rapidly turned to gas
    and poured out through the holes

JUDGE:
    How long did it take the gas
    to kill

7TH WITNESS:
    That depended on the amount used
    For reasons of economy usually
    a less than adequate amount was poured in
    so that the killing
    could take as long as five minutes

JUDGE:
    What was the immediate effect of the gas

7TH WITNESS:
    It induced dizziness and severe nausea
    and made breathing extremely difficult

JUDGE:
    How long was the room kept under gas

7TH WITNESS:
    20 minutes
    Then the ventilation system was turned on

and the gas pumped out
30 minutes later the doors were opened
But there was still gas
caught in small pockets
among the dead
which caused a dry hacking cough
For this reason
the men in the Clearance Detail
had to wear gas masks

JUDGE:

Did you
see this room after the door
had been opened

7TH WITNESS:

Yes
The corpses lay piled on top of each other
near the door and around the columns
Babies children and the sick at the bottom
Women above them
And at the very top the strongest men
The reason for this
was that the people trampled
and climbed on each other
because the gas initially spread
most thickly at floor level
The people clawing each other
were stuck together
Their skin was torn
Many were bleeding from nose and mouth
The faces were swollen
and spotted
The heaps of people were befouled
with vomit
excrement urine and menstrual blood
The Clearance Detail came in with hoses
and washed the corpses down

Then they were pulled
into the freight elevators
and taken up to the ovens
JUDGE:
How large were these elevators
7TH WITNESS:
There were two of them
each with a capacity of 25 dead
When one load was in
a bell was rung
to signal the Lugging Detail
that was standing by with carts
on the floor above
They had thongs
that they slipped over the wrists of the dead
The corpses were then lugged in the carts
to the ovens on a special track
Blood was washed away
by a steady stream of water
Before cremation
men of the Special Commando
conducted a final search
Every ornament still
to be found on the bodies
was removed
bracelets
neck chains
rings
earrings
Then the hair was cut off
and immediately bundled
and packed
Finally
the teeth extractors set to work
They were a crew picked
from first-class specialists

at Dr Mengele's express command
Still when they started in
with their crowbars and tongs
they tore out not only gold teeth
and bridges
but whole chunks of jaw
These pieces of bone and attached flesh
were thrown into an acid vat
to be eaten away
100 men worked continually
in two shifts
at the ovens

JUDGE:

How many ovens were there
in the crematorium

7TH WITNESS:

There were five ovens each
in the big crematoriums II and III
Each oven had three incinerating chambers
Beside these two crematoriums
at the end of the Arrival Platform
there were crematoriums IV and V
each with two four-chambered ovens
These two were set off about
800 yards back of the birch grove
When the operation was going full blast
46 incinerating chambers
were fired up

JUDGE:

How many bodies
could be put into one chamber

7TH WITNESS:

From three to five bodies
could be put in one chamber
However it was rare
that all ovens operated at one time

since they were often damaged
by overheating

JUDGE:

How long did cremation take
in an oven chamber

7TH WITNESS:

Approximately an hour
Then it could take a new load
In crematoriums II and III
more than 3000 people were cremated
in less than 24 hours
If the ovens were overcrowded
corpses were also burned in a ditch
that had been dug outside the building
These ditches were
about 100 feet long
and 20 feet deep
At each end there were drainage trenches
for the fat
The fat was ladled up in cans
and poured over the corpses
to make them burn faster
In the summer of 1944
when the cremations reached their peak
up to 20,000 people
were destroyed
daily
Their ashes were trucked off
to a river a mile and a half away
and dumped into the water

JUDGE:

What was done with the valuables
and gold fillings

1ST WITNESS:

When the clothes were collected
money and ornaments found among them

were dropped into a slot in the top
of a locked crate
Guards filled their own pockets first
Clothes and shoes
that the prisoners themselves
had carefully bundled together
were sent home
for the benefit of people
bombed out of their houses
Gold fillings were melted down
I was called in as examining magistrate
because packages sent from the camp
containing gold by the pound
had been confiscated
In the course of my investigation
I ascertained that this was dental gold
Calculating from the weight
of a single filling
I came to the conclusion
that thousands of people were required
to supply even one such nugget

JUDGE:

Do you mean
that even in those times
a magistrate was called in from outside
to conduct an investigation in the camp

1ST WITNESS:

Somewhere some idea of justice
still survived
The commanding officer
wanted to combat corruption in the camp
At the time of my visit there
he complained
that the men under his command
frequently failed to rise to the demands
made on them by their hard work

Then he took me to a crematorium installa-
    tion
where he explained
everything to me in great detail
Inside in the cremation rooms eveything
was polished to a shine
There was nothing to indicate
that people were cremated there
There wasn't even a speck of their dust
on the oven panels
The guards in their room sat
on a bench half drunk
and in the service room
women prisoners
especially picked for their beauty
were baking potato dumplings
which they served the men
When I made a search of their lockers
they proved
to contain a fortune
As judge I instituted proceedings
for theft
and some of them were arrested
and sentenced

JUDGE:
    How were these proceedings carried out
1ST WITNESS:
    It was a mock trial
    You could go up only so high
    and it was impossible
    to institute proceedings
    for multiple murder
JUDGE:
    As examining magistrate
    you saw no means
    of making your findings public

1ST WITNESS:
>   Before what court
>   could I have brought an action
>   for the killings of masses of people
>   and the seizure of their goods and property
>   by the highest administrative offices
>   I could not institute proceedings
>   against the government itself

JUDGE:
>   Was there no other way
>   of acting on this matter

1ST WITNESS:
>   I knew
>   no one would have believed
>   what I had to say
>   I would have been executed
>   or at the very least
>   locked up in an asylum
>   I considered fleeing the country
>   but I doubted whether
>   even abroad
>   anyone would believe me
>   and I asked myself what would happen
>   if I were believed
>   and I were called upon to testify
>   against my own people
>   and I could only conclude
>   that this my people would be destroyed
>   for its deeds
>   So I stayed

THE SONG OF THE FIRE OVENS

III

JUDGE:
 There has been testimony of an uprising
 carried out by the Special Commando
 When did this uprising occur
7TH WITNESS:
 On October 6 1944
 The Commando was to be liquidated
 by the guards that day
JUDGE:
 Did the Commando know this beforehand
7TH WITNESS:
 They all knew
 they were going to be killed
 Weeks before
 they had obtained cans of explosives
 from prisoners who worked
 in the armaments factory
 The plan was
 to first take care of the guards
 then blow up the crematoriums
 and escape
 But the crematorium
 where the explosives were stored
 blew up earlier than planned
 and many of the men
 went up with it
 There was a battle

but they were all overpowered
Hundreds of prisoners lay
face down on the ground
behind the birch grove
The men from the Political Division
shot them in the back of the head

JUDGE:

Which of the accused were present

7TH WITNESS:

Boger was in charge

JUDGE:

Was this crematorium
destroyed by the explosion

7TH WITNESS:

The explosion from four barrels of dynamite
blew up one entire building

JUDGE:

What happened to the other crematoriums

7TH WITNESS:

They were blown up
by staff personnel shortly after
The front was getting close

PROSECUTING ATTORNEY:

Does the witness
find it credible
that the adjutant
of the camp's commanding officer
was not informed
about what went on in the crematoriums

7TH WITNESS:

No
It was impossible
Each one of the 6000 camp staff personnel
knew what was taking place
and each at his post did
what was required

for the functioning of the whole
Furthermore every locomotive engineer
every switchman
every railroad employee
who had anything to do
with the transportation of the people
knew what went on in the camp
Every telegraph clerk and typist
who passed on the Deportation Orders
knew
Every single one
of the hundreds and
thousands of office workers
connected with the widespread operation
knew
what it was all about
COUNSEL FOR THE DEFENSE:
We object to these statements
which are dictated by sheer hate
Hate must never
form the basis
for a judgment
of the particulars under consideration here
7TH WITNESS:
I do not speak from hate
I have no desire for revenge
I am not concerned here
with the individual accused
but only wish to bring to mind
that what they did
could not have been carried out
without the support
of millions of others
COUNSEL FOR THE DEFENSE:
This proceeding is strictly confined

to what can be substantiated by proof
against our clients
General charges
are irrelevant
Especially charges
directed against an entire nation
which at that time was engaged
in a great and sacrificial war

7TH WITNESS:

I only
want to point out if I may
how many spectators lined the way
when we were driven from our homes
and loaded into freight cars
The accused in these proceedings
were only the last
in a long line

PROSECUTING ATTORNEY:

Can the witness
tell us how many people
in his estimation
were killed
in total
in the camp

7TH WITNESS:

Of the 9 million 600 thousand persecuted
who lived in the regions
ruled by their persecutors
6 million have disappeared
and it can be taken for granted
that most of them
were deliberately destroyed
Those who were not shot
beaten to death
tortured to death

or gassed
died of hunger disease and misery
or of being worked to death
Yet to arrive at the sum total
of the defenseless sacrificed
in this war of extermination
we must add to the 6 million
killed for racial reasons
3 million Russian prisoners of war
shot or starved to death
as well as the 10 million civilians
of the occupied countries
who perished
COUNSEL FOR THE DEFENSE:
Even though we all feel
most deeply for the victims
still it is our duty here
to counter and oppose
all exaggerations
and vilification
originating from certain parties
In relation to this camp
not even the sum of 2 million dead
can be conclusively established
Only the death of several hundred thousand
can be proven
The majority of the groups named
ended up in the east
and those seized
and liquidated
as armed units
cannot be counted among the murdered
nor can those who deserted
to enemy armies and fell in battle
During the course of these proceedings

it has become all too clear
which political point of view
has determined
the accusations of the witnesses
accusations which the witnesses certainly
had sufficient time
to work out among themselves
  [*The Accused laugh nodding in
  agreement*]

PROSECUTING ATTORNEY:

This is a willful and conscious expression
of contempt
for those who died in the camp
and for those survivors
who have appeared here
to testify as witnesses
The behavior of the counsel for the defense
clearly demonstrates the persistence
of that same outlook
of which the accused present were guilty

COUNSEL FOR THE DEFENSE:

Who is this assistant prosecutor
with his unsuitable clothes
It is I believe a Middle European custom
to appear in court with a closed robe

JUDGE:

The court calls for order
Accused Mulka
will you now tell us
what you knew
about the Extermination Program
and what orders you issued
in this connection

ACCUSED #1:

I issued no orders connected with that

270

JUDGE:
  You knew nothing
  about the Extermination Program
ACCUSED #1:
  Only toward the end of my time in the service
  I can say now
  that I was filled with revulsion
JUDGE:
  If this was the case
  why did you not refuse
  to participate
ACCUSED #1:
  I was an officer
  and knew the military penal code
PROSECUTING ATTORNEY:
  You were not an officer
ACCUSED #1:
  I certainly was
PROSECUTING ATTORNEY:
  You were not an officer
  You belonged to a uniformed
  Murder Commando
ACCUSED #1:
  You are attacking my honor
PROSECUTING ATTORNEY:
  Accused Mulka
  we are dealing with murder
ACCUSED #1:
  We were convinced
  that our orders
  were all part of achieving some secret
  military objective
  Mr President I almost broke down
  The whole business made me so sick I
  had to be hospitalized
  But I want to make it clear

that I only looked on from the outside
and that I
kept my own hands out of it
Your Honor I was against
the whole thing
I myself was
persecuted by the system

JUDGE:

What happened to you

ACCUSED #1:

I was arrested
because I had expressed
defeatist opinions
I was in prison for three months
After my release
I was caught in an enemy attack
As an old soldier
I was able to save many lives
by helping with the evacuations
My own son was killed
Mr President at this trial
the millions who also lost their lives
for their own country
should not be forgotten
and what happened after the war
shouldn't be forgotten either
and all the things
that are still being done against us
All of us
I want to make that very clear
did nothing but our duty
even when that duty was hard
and even when it grieved us to do it
Today
when our nation has worked its way up
after a devastating war

to a leading position in the world
we ought to concern ourselves
with other things
than blame and reproaches
that should be thought of
as long since atoned for
     [Loud approbation from the Accused]

Winner of the 1965-66 Season
New York
Drama Critics' Circle
and Tony Awards
now a UNITED ARTISTS
picture.

75178/75c

THE PERSECUTION
AND ASSASSINATION
OF JEAN PAUL MARAT
AS PERFORMED BY THE INMATES
OF THE ASYLUM OF CHARENTON
UNDER THE DIRECTION
OF THE MARQUIS DE SADE
by PETER WEISS

"...extraordinary...literally staggering...
one of the most powerful books I have ever read...."
—RICHARD KLUGER, EDITOR, New York Herald Tribune Book Week

THE
PAINTED
BIRD

Jerzy Kosinski

95037/95¢